Sustainable Human Development in the North-Eastern Region of India

By

J.B. Ganguly

Regency Publications
New Delhi-110 008

Division of
DAYA PUBLISHING HOUSE
4760-61/23, Ansari Road,
Darya Ganj, New Delhi - 110 002
Phone: 23245578, 23244987; Fax: (011) 23260116
E-mail: info@regency-books.com
Website: www.regencybooks.com

ISBN 81-86030-29-8

Published by Regency Publications, 20/36-G, Old Market, West Patel Nagar, New Delhi 110 008 for Indian Council of Social Science Research—North-Eastern Regional Centre, Shillong, and Printed at Radiant Printers, New Delhi 110 008, Phones: 571 3968, 578 3571.

In Loving Memory
of My Grandson
Saurav

Foreword

The present study is based on the text of three lectures delivered by Professor J.B. Ganguly at the North-Eastern Regional Centre of the Indian Council of Social Science Research in March 1995. The NERC has instituted annual lecture series on the broad theme of 'Development and Social Change' and these lectures are the third in the series. We are thankful to Professor Ganguly for kindly accepting our invitation to deliver these lectures.

Professor Ganguly is a distinguished economist and after retiring as Vice-chancellor of Tripura University now lives in Calcutta. Being earnestly concerned about the prospects of development in North-Eastern Region of India, he brings his experience to advocate an alternative paradigm of development shaking off the stereotyped notion that there is no alternative for peace and development in northeast. We hope that these lectures in published form will not only attract the attention of the theoretician but provide fairly good insight to the policy planners and enlightened public.

January, 1996

M.N. Karna
Honorary Director
ICSSR-NERC
Shillong

Preface

The process of planned development of the North Eastern Region has been in progress since the early 1950's. Considerable progress in the spread of literacy and educational attainments has been achieved. People's access to medical and health care facilities has also been expanded. Development of the basic infrastructure—new roads and railway lines, generation of more power, extension of transport and communication (including telecommunication) facilities to more and remoter areas—has been opening up the possibilities of achieving further social and economic development. And this region is yet far behind many other regions of the country in these respects. Therefore the process of development of these services and facilities needs to be carried forward. But it is also now time to take stock of the impact that these changes are having on the human mind and spirit.

An important gain has been the enlargement of people's choices and opportunities. Throughout the North East a robust creed of humanism is perceptible, many individuals are confident of reaching self-fulfilment on their own. The world view of the people has been widening at a rapid pace. Contacts with other people are multiplying. Market forces have been penetrating into their system making all transactions more and more impersonal. Many traditional institutions and even values have been falling apart. More and more people are losing their cultural moorings. As a counter-development several ethnic communities are now bent on asserting their ethnic identity. And many parts of the North East are now the scenes of ethnic violence, secessionist revolt and insurgency. The ongoing process of development as a result has got a setback.

In fact the paradigm of development being followed is inappropriate, inequitous and unsustainable. The centralization of decision-making process in bringing about planned development has severely eroded the role of the grassroot organization and the egalitarian ethos of ensuring equitable access of every household to resources like land, forests and water courses, etc. for productive activities. Easy flow of money for implementing exogenously formulated development schemes and other projects has been killing the spirit of self-help and even generating corruption in social life. The region's natural resources are being depleted at a fast rate, biodiversity is being lost and dependence of the rural and tribal masses on the bio-mass to meet many of their daily needs is in jeopardy. Sustainable use of resources for bringing improvement in people's living standard is becoming more and more difficult. The main beneficiaries are the contractors, businessmen and local vested interests. Economic stratification of the local communities is on the increase. It is urgently needed that the development process is decentralized and community organizations empowered to carry out people-centered plan schemes embodying the principle of sustainable use of resources.

Being earnestly concerned about the prospects of development and peace in the North Eastern Region, I am convinced that an alternative paradigm of development needs to be adopted shaking off the so-called TINA (there is no alternative) mindset prevalent in the country. The model of sustainable human development as formulated by the United Nationas Development Programme appears to be an appropriate model for India as well the North East and it is an endorsement of the Nehru model of highlighting the principle: "People should develop along the lines of their own genius and we should avoid imposing anything on them." This model provides for economic growth with equity; regeneration of environment rather than depleting it; enpowerment of the communities in place of marginalizing them. Development process is pro-people, pro-nature, pro-jobs and pro-women.

In the North East some progress has been achieved in the development of the social sector but much more has to be done for raising the income of the people, providing jobs for all, improving the status of women and preserving biodiversity.

I have been so much committed to this approach to planned development that when I was invited by the North Eastern Regional Centre of the Indian Council of Social Science Research, Shillong to deliver a series of three lectures under their Annual Lecture series on the development and social change I readily accepted it to be able to share my ideas with the teachers, students and scholars in the North Eastern Hill University and other invited guests particularly, Prof. B. Pakem, VC, NEHU, Prof. M.N. Karna Hon. Director and Dr. C.J. Thomas, Asst. Director of NERC. I am grateful to the NERC of ICSSR and the NEHU authorities for providing me with this opportunity. I have been overwhelmed by the response that I got from the audience to the ideas I spelled out in the three lectures. The original lectures have been revised and enlarged in the light of the discussion that followed the delivery of each lecture.

Contents

List of Tables

Chapter 1

The Concept of Sustainable Human Development

The Genesis of the Concept

Spectacular development in the field of science and technology has given humankind tremendous power of harnessing natural resources, particularly the 'free energy locked in fossil fuels' for increasing production of material goods and services. This power is not evenly distributed between countries. Those countries which acquired mastery over this power became the industrialized and rich countries of the north. They represent only 20 per cent of the world's total population. Motivated by the belief that resources did not place any limit on the capacity to produce more goods and guided by the ideology of 'more is better' these countries have been producing and consuming more and more by using up fossil fuels at a very fast rate 'leading to global pollution, climate and sea-level change.'

This process has been encouraged by the Neoclassical economic growth model propounding the possibility of achieving steady-state economic growth on a sustained basis. Very briefly this theoretical construction may be stated as follows:

In the production of goods and services the various factors of production are used. For simplification of analysis let the number of factors or inputs be taken as two, namely, capital and labour. It is presumed that the factors of production are substitutable for one another without any limit. And the scarce resource is substituted by the abundant one depending on their relative prices. As a resource becomes relatively scarce its relative price rises. Therefore the tendency will be to employ more of the abundant resource price of which is lower. This will lead to a change in the capital-labour ratio in production which will entail a change in the technology of production. Growth of labour supply depends on the growth of population and productivity of labour depends on technical progress. It has, therefore, been explained that the rates of growth of population and technical progress ultimately determine the longrun rate of economic growth.

Based on such premises the economists have worked out several versions of 'golden age' of growth by which is meant a state of dynamic equilibrium which can be continuously maintained by achieving the desired rate of accumulation of capital given the rates of growth of population and output per labour which depends on the rate of technical progress. This ushers in the so-called 'golden age' because starting from a state of full employment or near full employment 'and a composition of the stock of capital appropriate to the desired rate of accumulation,' as explained by Joan Robinson, output and income go on growing continuously while maintaining the state of full or near full employment in the country. This implies that, there are no ups and downs in economic activities and no cyclical unemployment and misery. Also, in such a state of steady state growth per capita consumption grows at the maximum rate which is the equilibrium rate. This situation has been equated with maximum social welfare which the people enjoy ever after.

The basic premise of such constructions of static and dynamic equilibria is that human welfare depends on material wealth and that welfare grows as the acquisition of material wealth grows. And there is no limit to growth of production of goods and services as there is no absolute scarcity of resources required for production though there may be relative scarcity. But a relively scarce resource can always be substituted by a relatively abundant one. The competitive market mechanism brings about the optimum allocation of resources for production of goods and services and also the distribution of output or income among the different factors of production according to their respective contributions to the total output.

The utopian concept of the possibility of enjoying increasing level of consumption without any limit is a physical impossibility. According to the First Law of Thermodynamics total quantum of matter and energy is fixed. Production of goods and services means transformation of matter and energy from one form to the other. The Second Law of Thermodynamics (increasing entropy) implies that such transformation leads to disorganization and dissipation of energy causing the total amount of usable energy to fall although the total amount of energy as such remains unchanged. Energy once used up cannot be recycled. Such a limitation ultimately also applies to materials which can be recycled, it is true, but never to the extent of cent per cent; a part of the materials is irrevocably lost in each stage of use.

The dangers of depletion of natural resources and abuses of the environment on account of growing 'industrialism and population' is ultimately explainable in terms of the entropy law. Leaving aside the concern about the ultimate heat death of the universe (when the quantum of usable energy will be nil as the total quantity of energy falls below the usable level as a result of disorganization and so becomes useless) we are to take note of the entropy law for our immediate guidance to action. Herman E. Daly brings out the fact most effectively in the following words (1977 : 110) :

"The effect of the entropy law is as immediate and concrete as the facts that you can't burn the same tank of gasoline twice, that organisms cannot live in a medium of their own waste products, and that efficiencies cannot reach, much less exceed, 100 per cent. The low entropy of highly organized stocks of wealth and human bodies must be maintained by the continual importation of low-entropy inputs from the environment and the continual exportation of high-entropy outputs back to the environment, where through the agency of solar-powered biogeochemical cycles they are transformed into low-entropy forms on varying time scales. The entropic flow, beginning with depletion and ending with pollution (the throughput), is the necessary cost of maintaining the stocks of commodities and people. Too large a throughput can disrupt the biosphere and impair its capacity to assimilate wastes. . . . this entropic degradation is a cost and must be reckoned as a cost and minimized for any chosen level of population and per capita wealth."

Even without going into such fundamentals, a number of scholars and authorities in the sixties and seventies voiced their concerns about the conflict between 'the finite environment and an ever-increasing demand on that by growing industrialism and population.' In the U.S.A. Rachel Carson published her book, "Silent Spring" in 1962 which set a large number of Americans expressing their words of caution against the process of environmental degradation, exhaustion of natural resources at a fast rate and the fall in the carrying capacity of earth on account of high rates of growth of population in the developing countries. The 'Club of Rome' organized by the Italian economist and businessman A. Peccei brought out publications like "The Predicament of Mankind", "Where Are We Going?", etc. One of the most referred to works is "The Limits to Growth" sponsored by the Club of Rome and written by noted scholars led by D.H. Meadows. The American biologist B. Commons wrote "The Closing Circle" to bring out the threat of ecological disasters of the on-going development process. These works represent expressions of concern about the bleak prospects of human survival in the long run unless appropriate measures are taken to avoid overtaxing of the environment upon which the human life and society depend.

Daly has even propounded an impossibility theorem to explain that there is a limit on the number of 'person-years' of high consumption of industrial life-style as in the U.S.A. (1979 : 38). Contesting the contention of many growth economists that this difficulty could be overcome by technological improvements he points out that many of the so-called technological triumphs fail the first test of not 'increasing costs of other users either now or in the future'. Quoting Aldo Leopold, Daly points out that the technical improvements of the recent past represent "improvements in the pump, rather than the well" (*op cit.* : 45).

The emphasis laid on achieving growth even in rich countries is an attempt at evading the compulsion of reducing inequality in the distribution of income and wealth for avoiding social conflict. But with the passing of time the prognostications made by the physical and social scientists about the dangers of the on-going pattern of resource use particularly in the industrialized west have been convincing more and more people that technology cannot resolve the problem of finiteness of the environment and that humankind's future is vitally linked up with the achievement of conservation of natural resources and protecting the environment from pollution which has been threatening the very life-support system of the space ship earth.

International Awareness and Actions

Adverse consequences of environmental degradation like global warming, ozone depletion, water pollution, destruction of bio-diversity, etc. do not remain confined to any particular country or group of countries. These problems have global dimensions and conservation of the global commons implies international understanding and cooperation. Therefore, the UNO became involved in mobilizing world opinion in favour of conservation of resources and protection of the environment through actions both at the national and international levels. With this end in view the United Nations Conference on the Human Environment was organized in 1972 at Stockholm, Sweden. Both the developed and developing nations participated in the conference and highlighted the problems faced by them respectively and agreed that international cooperation was needed to address the problem. From this conference emerged the concept of "eco-development" which 'focused on the satisfaction of basic needs in an environmentally sound production system. The achievement of self-reliance needed for such a production system was the basis of eco-development approach' (Nayar 1994, p. 1327).

In the later half of the eighties a definite shift in the approach of developed countries to address the environmental issues took place. They were not interested in promoting self-reliant growth in the developing countries in order to ensure protection of the environment. It was asserted that the high rate of growth of population in the third world countries was the root cause of persistent mass poverty and the consequent environmental degradation. These factors combine to make the process of development unsustainable in these countries. Achievement of sustainable development by checking the growth of population and restricting the use of natural resources within the permissible limit set by the carrying capacity of a given territory should, therefore, be the main agenda of action for environment management. The International Union for the Conservation of Energy formulated the World Conservation Strategy in 1980 in which the concept of sustainable development was first spelled out (Nayar, *ibid*, p. 1329). The World Commission of Environment and Development set up by the UN General Assembly submitted its report entitled "Our Common Future" which was adopted by the General Assembly in 1987. This report highlighted the idea of sustainable development as an approach to environment management. Sustainable development implies "meeting the needs of the present without compromising the ability of future generations to meet their own needs."

The north-south dialogues on measures for conserving and enhancing the earth's resources, that is, achieving sustainable development through mutual cooperation have taken place in several international conferences and on world fora. But a commonly agreed agenda of effective actions are yet to evolve. The paradigm of sustainable development needs to be interpreted in more meaningful terms. The deliberations held in the Earth Summit held in Rio de Janerio emphasized the fact that the process of development to be sustainable should be socially equitable, ecologically viable and, of course, economically efficient (Gowarikar and Sachs 1994, p. 1383). The concept of sustainable development should also subsume the concept of sustainable consumption. The United Nations Environment Programme has drawn attention to the fact that "current consumption pattern in developed countries are not sustainable, because their global duplication would cause intolerable impacts on natural resources, public health and our sustaining ecosystem". Principle 8 of the 1992 Rio Declaration on Environment and Development also states:

"To achieve sustainable development and a higher quality of life for all people, states should reduce and eliminate unsustainable patterns of production and consumption, and promote appropriate demographic policies".

According to the UNEP, "a possible working definition for sustainable consumption means the provision of services, and related products, which respond to basic needs and bring a better quality of life, while minimizing the use of natural resources and toxic materials as well as the emissions of waste and pollutants over the life cycle of the service or product with a view not to jeopardize the needs of future generations." (UNEP, Elements For Policies For sustainable Consumption as quoted in the Report on the Symposium on Sustainable Consumption held at Oslo, Norway, 19–20 January 1994).

The perception of development has changed in the recent years. Earlier the emphasis was on 'economic' development, now it is on 'human' development. The United Nations Development Programme has been publishing annually since 1990 reports on human development in all the countries of the world. The concept of human development emphasizes the fact that people must be at the centre of all development. In its HDR for 1992 the UNDP enlarged the concept of human development as 'sustainable human development' to highlight the need for having the process of development that is economically, socially and ecologically sustainable. "That is, current consumption cannot be financed by incurring debts that others must repay in the future. Investment must be made in the health and education of today's population so as not to create a social debt for future generations. And natural resources must be used in ways that do not create ecological debts by over-exploiting the carrying and productive capacity of the earth": (p. 17). The concept has been further elaborated in the 1994 HDR 9 p. 4): "In the final analysis, sustainable human development is pro-people, pro-jobs and pro-nature. It gives the highest priority to poverty reduction, productive employment and environmental regeneration."

The principle of sustainability is vitally linked with the principle of equity both at the national and international levels. The poor sections of the society are constrained to overuse their environment for eking out an existence. For them the problems of global warming or depletion of the ozone layer have little meaning. They are vitally affected by, what the UNDP has termed, 'silent emergencies', namely, polluted water, degraded forests and land and environmental diseases, etc. For them 'what is at risk is not the quality of life but life itself'. And if poverty cannot be removed, environmental sustainability cannot be achieved.

The strategies for achieving sustainable human development at the national level must be so formulated as to reduce poverty, create employment opportunities and strengthen social integration. For alleviating poverty the state must provide (i) basic social services like basic education and primary health care for the poor, (ii) carry out land reform measures for ensuring equitable distribution of land and agricultural resources, (iii) extend credit supply facilities to all those who need this important input for production, (iv) expand employment opportunities so that everyone can have sustainable livelihood and (v) build up a social safety net 'to catch those whom markets exclude' (*ibid*, p. 20). The basic requirement for the success of anti-poverty strategy is that it must be decentralized and participatory. "The poor cannot benefit from economic development if they do not even participate in its design" (*ibid*). For creation of employment opportunities for all adequate investment should be made in education and skill formation of the people, necessary physical infrastructure built up, stable macro-economic policies followed to maintain a favourable climate for investment, labour-intensive technologies followed in developing countries having comparative supply of abundant labour, creation of employment possibilities by organizing public works programme and special measures taken by the government for the benefit of the disadvantaged groups, such as women and weaker sections of the society.

To realize the goal of enabling all ethnic groups to actively and effectively participate in productive activities for achieving sustainable livelihood for all an important policy strategy must be to promote the process of social integration. For this purpose besides ensuring equality before law for all, protecting minority rights and culture, eradicating all kinds of discrimination against any group, special measures should be taken to expand educational facilities and employment opportunities particularly for the most disadvantaged and marginalized groups including women. Ultimately, of course, the sure way of enhancing social integration is to decentralize administrative functions and to enable the people to directly participate in running grass-roots organizations.

The new paradigm of development formulated by the UNDP "also recognizes that not much can be achieved without a dramatic improvement in the status of women and the opening of all opportunities to women" (*ibid* : 4).

The concept of sustainable human development has a global dimension. A new global ethic should inform the building up of an equitable world order. The world is sharply divided into rich nations having one-fourth of the world population and the poor nations accounting for the remaining three-fourths. One-fourth of the world population is even deprived of the basic human needs while the rich nations consume four-fifths of humanity's natural capital without paying for it. Environmental sustainability implies maintaining the health of the global commons. All nations must take concerted actions for preserving the global commons. The present pattern of sharing the environment as a cost-free resource has enabled the rich nations not to bother about conserving the environment. These nations have been mostly responsible for polluting the environment. The UNDP has estimated that if "the environment were correctly priced and tradable permits were issued to all nations (50% on the basis of GDP and 50% on the basis of population), the rich nations might have to transfer as much as 5% of their combined GDP to the poor nations" (ibid p. 19). Through such transfer of consumption abilities from the rich to the poor nations a move towards achieving some global balance in the use of environmental resource may be made. In the ultimate analysis, the ideology of shared responsibility for global sustainability cannot be isolated from the ideology of shared global prosperity.

India's Approach to Sustainable Development and Achievement: An Appraisal

The Government of India had adopted the policy of conservation of resources and protection of the environment in the early seventies. At the Stockholm Conference in 1972, Mrs. Gandhi, the then Prime Minister, emphatically pointed out that 'poverty was the greatest pollutant' and that for removal of poverty a 'non-exploitative strategy of development' should be pursued. She further asserted that the objective of achieving development and that of protecting the environment were not contradictory but complementary. Later she formulated the government's policy of achieving 'rapid economic development without ecological damage'. In keeping with this goal, the National Committee of Environment Planning and Coordination was constituted in 1972. "In 1980 an expert committee headed by Narayan Dutt Tiwari, the then Union Minister of Planning, recommended that a department of environment be created at the centre; environment advisers be appointed in the different ministries, who would assess and monitor the ecological consequences of development policies and projects; and that a national committee on environment planning be set up to serve as a 'think-tank' to go into the problems of conservation and to suggest remedial measures, etc."

The National Committee on Environment Planning and Coordination brought out the alarming proportions of environmental degradation and destruction of land and water resources in its draft report published in 1981. It revealed that " of the total land area of 304 million hectares, over 175 million hectares were environmentally endangered, due to deforestation, erosion and water-logging. The area affected by floods had doubled from 20 million hectares in 1971 to 40 million hectares entailing an average loss of Rs. 700 crores. Only 12 per cent of the land surface was under adequate forest cover as against the target of 33 per cent by the 1952 national forest policy" (Suraiya, 1984).

This report alerted the Government for taking steps against environmental degradation in the country and the Department of Environment was established in 1981 for dealing with the environmental issues. The creation of this department made it possible for the Government to undertake several measures and projects for addressing the problems of environmental degradation in acceptance of the concept of eco-development as formulated and recommended for adoption by all member countries in the 1972 Stockholm Conference on Environment and Development. This concept "focused on the satisfaction of basic needs in an environmentally sound production system. The achievement of self-reliance needed for such a production system was the basis of eco-development approach" (Nayar, 1994, p. 1327).

The concern for environmental conservation even as the process of social and economic growth and development should be maintained was reflected in the Sixth Five Year Plan (1980–85) document. It was stated therein that in preparing plans and programmes a crucial guiding dimension must be an assessment of their impacts on the environment. The two kinds of environmental problems faced by India, according to the Planning Commission, were people's poverty and underdevelopment on the one hand and the negative effects of the very process of development on the other. In its words: "The first category has to do with the impact on the health and integrity of our natural resources (land, soil, water, forests, wildlife, etc.) as a result of poverty and the inadequate availability, for a large section of our population, of the means to fulfil basic human needs (food, fuel, shelter, employment, etc.). The second category has to do with the unintended side effects to achieve rapid economic growth and development" (The Sixth Five Year Plan (1980–85), p. 343).

Categorizing the specific areas of environmental and eco-development problems in the country the Planning Commission highlighted the "colossal damage done by the denudation of the Himalayas and other watersheds to our water resources," the rate of deforestation, extinction of some species of ecosystems, increasing rate of pollution of environment, etc. To check the process of such ecological deterioration and to conserve effectively the country's rich biodiversity the Planning Commission formulated the programmes of eco-development. In doing so it presumed that without checking the rate of growth of population and enabling the people to meet their basic needs and improving the quality of their life, the environmental health of the country cannot be truly protected. Even as in this sense the very planning of national development promotes the cause of environmental conservation, specific programmes are required to be undertaken for correcting numerous local and regional stresses on environmental resources which result from the prevailing conditions of poverty and underdevelopment and from 'the unintended side-effects of programmes for national development.'

The policy of conservation of land, water, forests, biodiversity and checking of environmental pollution, etc. for eco-development ultimately aims at ensuring sustainable use of resources. And the Government of India's approach to sustainable development emphasizes the alleviation of poverty of the masses as the best guarantee for protection of environment. At the same time the necessity for adoption of specific programmes of action and legislative measures for protection of environment was also underlined.

In accordance with this policy the Department of Environment was entrusted with the work of undertaking environmental appraisal of different development projects proposed for inclusion in the plan. The department also monitored the level of environmental pollution and working of regulatory measures for pollution control, conservation of diverse bio-resources, marine eco-system, etc.

The work of this department expanded over the years. Therefore it was upgraded into a ministry in the

Government of India under the name of Ministry of Environment, Forest and Wildlife in 1985. In the following year the Environment Protection Act was passed to empower the Government to coordinate the functions of the statutory and other agencies involved in environmental protection at the central and state levels. The setting up of the National Wasteland Development Board in 1985 was another step in coordinating and monitoring schemes of waste land development and robust afforestation programmes in the country. Similarly the Ganga Action Plan was initiated in 27 cities to make this great river system free from pollution. In India's planning system it is now a compulsory requirement that environmental impact assessment studies are made in respect of all projects which are required to be cleared by the Government/Planning Commission. Sanctions of projects, be it river valley development, power generation—hydel, thermal or atomic—setting up of mining or industrial units or development of ports and harbours or even urban land-use, etc. are given only after a project is cleared after making such studies.

The integration of the concept of eco-development in the formulation and implementation of the Five Year Plans of the country reflected, by implication, the Government's upholding the concept of sustainable human development. Much before the United Nations Development Programme propagated the concept of human development in 1990, that is, when the First Five Year Plan of India was prepared in 1951 by the Planning Commission, it was stated that the objective of planned development would be "to open to all people opportunities for a richer and more varied life." This is indeed the essence of the idea of human development as defined by the UNDP. According to this definition the objective of development should be to expand human capabilities and enlarge the range of people's choices.

The concept of sustainable development, in the sense that harmonious interdependent relations between man and nature should be maintained while the growth of national output is achieved, was enshrined in India's planning process at the time of preparing the Fourth Plan (1969–74). In the Fourth Five Year Plan it was stated:

> "The physical environment is a dynamic, complex and inter-connected system in which any action in one part affects others. There is also the interdependence of living things and their relationships with land, air and water. Planning for harmonious development recognizes this unity of nature and man. Such planning is possible only on the basis of a comprehensive appraisal of issues —particularly economic and ecological .... It is necessary, therefore, to introduce the environmental aspects into our planning and development. Along with effective conservation and rational use of natural resources, protection and improvement of human environment is vital for national well-being. It is particularly important that long-term basic considerations, the social costs and benefits be used as the yardstick rather than private gains and losses" (Quoted in Raza, 1990, p. 27).

Of course, the goal of sustainable development as such was formally adopted as the development policy of the country in 1992. In that year the Ministry of Environment and Forests, Government of India submitted to Parliament the National Conservation Strategy and Policy Statement on Environment and Development. The concept of sustainable development was the cornerstone of that policy statement. It explained that there was no real conflict between the goals of development and that of conservation of resources. It also laid stress on the removal of poverty through development, controlling the rate of growth of population and appropriate management of resource use or what may be termed as 'resourceful use of renewable resources' for realizing the goal of sustainable development.

The Approach to the Eighth Plan (1990–95) document succinctly explained the objective of sustainable development as follows:

"... Improvements in the standards and quality of life of the people have to be based on sustenance of life support systems through conservation and regeneration of the natural resource base. The present generation owes this not only to itself but also to future generations and to myriad other species with which its survival is organically and irrevocably linked. What is needed is an ecological imagination that informs development thinking.

"... There should be more rigorous scrutiny of the environmental impact of every development scheme, and ecologically sustainable development accepted as an end in itself" (p. 44).

Even as the Planning Commission and the Government have been aware of the need for conservation of resources, actual performance has been far from satisfactory. As the Approach to the Eighth Plan admits:

"Deforestation, desertification, pollution of the atmosphere and of the rivers; fast depletion of water tables, and destruction of top soil have all affected the very survival of our people" (p. 43).

Clearly, faulty planning and management of resources and application of inappropriate technology and persistent poverty of the people have contributed to such environmental degradations and erosion of natural resource base.

We may have an idea of the status of India's natural resources balance sheet as culled from Human Development Report 1995 (p. 189) and given in Table 1.

The proportion of arable land to total land area is quite high in India, namely, 57%. Of course the whole of the arable land area is not actually under cultivation. The Agricultural Census of 1970–71 showed that 49.4 % of the total land area of the country was under agricultural operations.

Table 1 : India's Natural Resources Balance Sheet

1. Land area (1000 sq km), 1992	2973
2. Arable land (as % of land area), 1992	57.1
3. Irrigated land (as % of arable land area), 1992	27.0
4. Forest and woodland (as % of land area), 1992	23.0
5. Annual rate of deforestation : 1980–89(%)	2.3
6. Reforestation (1,000 ha per year): 1980–89	138
7. Internal renewable water resources per capita (1,000 cu m per year), 1992	3.1
8. Annual fresh water withdrawals (% of water resources): 1980–89	41

As the National Committee of Environment Planning and Coordination has pointed out (see p. 11 above), 175 million hectares or about 53% of the land area is environmentally endangered. This is really an alarming problem facing the country having a high rate of growth of population.

India's achievement in bringing arable land under irrigation is comparatively low. South Korea (64%), North Korea (72.3%), China (50.9%) and even Indonesia (36.7%) have higher proportions of arable land under irrigation than that of India which is only 27%. Annual fresh water withdrawals being 41% of total water resources, the potential of expanding the area under irrigation still remains to be fully realized.

Keeping of land under forest cover is an important means of conserving the land resource and protecting land from soil erosion. According to the National Forest Policy of 1988 a minimum of one-third (i.e., 33.33%) of the total land area of the country should be under forest or tree cover. "In the hills and mountainous regions," it says, "the aim should be to maintain two-third of the area under such cover in order to prevent erosion and land degradation and to ensure the stability of the fragile eco-system". The present position is quite disappointing since only 23% of the country's land area is under forest and woodland. What is of greater concern is that the annual rate of deforestation is 2.3%. As against that with the annual rate of reforestation of 138,000 hectares it will take quite a long time to reach the goal of bringing one-third of the land area under forest, if at all it is achieved.

The above facts clearly indicate that India has not been able to maintain, and far less to enhance, the stock of her basic natural resources like land, water and forest. But these resources need to be conserved with utmost efforts as the pressure on them has been increasing rapidly with the rise in population at a high rate. Though the rate of growth of population marginally declined from 2.22% during the 1971–81 decade to 2.14 % in the 1981–91 decade, it is still quite high. The UNDP has estimated that at the current growth rate (1992), India's population will be double by 2028 A.D. (Human Development Report, 1995, p. 187). According to the World Bank's Development Report, 1993, India's population is likely to rise from 866 million in 1991 to 1365 million by 2025. Even if we agree with this projection, it will mean that the pressure on land and other natural resources of the growing population will be extremely difficult to sustain unless an appropriate strategy is adopted for preserving and enhancing these resources and using them efficiently for productive purpose on a sustainable basis as also for substantially bringing down the rate of growth of population.

There have been various estimates of India's food needs for the future based on alternative projections of population growth and distribution of income and income-elasticity of demand for food. Food demands projected by Radhakrishna and Ravi for the years 2000 and 2010 amount to 205.26 and 250.21 million tonnes respectively as against that of 183.71 million tonnes in 1995 (Bhalla 1994: 5). Such tremendously increased needs for food will have to be met by our agriculture sector without jeopardizing the sustainability of the land and related resources.

Since the mid-1960's India has been depending on the so-called green revolution technology in achieving spectacular increases in food production in the country and thereby strengthening the food security system. Uses of high-yielding varieties of seeds, irrigation water, chemical fertilizers and pesticides have been the core input package of the new technology. But the application of heavy dozes of chemical fertilizers and pesticides as pest control measures have been causing environmental pollution and over-exploitation of underground water resource has been leading to rapid exhaustion of this valuable asset. The on-going green revolution technology has been damaging the soil structure quality and thereby seriously affecting the sustainability of the agricultural system.

Vandana Shiva (1993: 238) has accused that green revolution in agriculture "was primarily a recipe for introduction of monocultures and destruction of diversity. This was also linked to introduction of centralised control of agriculture and erosion of decentralised decion-making about agriculture and cropping patterns. Uniformity and centralisation made for social and ecological vulnerability and breakdown . . . ."

M.S. Swaminathan has, however, joined issue with the critics of the green revolution claiming that by raising per hectare productivity of foodgrains, the green revolution has saved much of our forests from being converted into farm lands in order to meet the additional demand for food. He cautions that slowing down of the process of agricultural intensification and diversification in our country will be socially disastrous. For, seventy per cent of our population is dependent on agriculture and allied activities including agro-industries. New opportunities for providing livelihood for additional eleven million persons will have to be created every year in India. And much of this burden will have to be borne by the agrarian sector. "Importing food and other agricultural commodities will hence have the same impact as importing unemployment. Thus what we need now is an environmentally sustainable and socially equitable green revolution—what may be termed an ever-green revolution" (The Hindu Magazine, Sunday, 21 May 1995).

Intensive cultivation of land without conservation of soil fertility and soil structure has been termed exploitative farming by Swaminathan. This will lead to desertification while irrigating farmlands without building proper drainage system will turn soil alkaline and saline. Indiscriminate use of pesticides, fungicides and herbicides will disturb biological balance and cause increasing incidences of cancer and other diseases. Over-tapping of underground water without appropriate provision for recharging the source will soon exhaust the reserve. He has also cautioned that the growing tendency of replacing "the numerous locally adapted varieties with one or two high-yielding strains in large contiguous areas would result in the spread of serious diseases capable of wiping out entire crops" (*ibid*). The existing trend of exploitative agriculture has been termed by Swaminathan as "Greed Revolution". He wants to get it replaced by 'sustainable green revolution' (or ever-green revolution) through the widespread adoption of what he calls ecotechnologies. "Ecotechnology involves", according to him, "the blending of the ecological prudence and technologies of the past, with the best in frontier technologies, particularly biotechnology, information technology, space technology, renewable energy technology and management technology. Without ecotechnological empowerment, farm-men and -women will not be able to produce more food and other agricultural commodities on an environmentally sustainable basis from less land, water and energy resources." (*ibid*).

Adoption of such technology will need 'appropriate packages of services and public policies.' Swaminathan even suggests the enactment of a National Food Security Act making it obligatory for the producers to adopt measures for conservation of land, water, forests, biodiversity and the protection of the atmosphere. Maintenance of adequate food security reserves must be also legally binding. The other aspects of the legal measure should be elimination of endemic hunger, adoption of better post-harvest technology, empowerment of the households to be entitled to equitable access to productive assets, employment, income, etc.

The objective of achieving sustainable development is based on the premise that it is quite possible for achieving growth of the Gross Domestic Product on a sustained basis while maintaining and enhancing the stock of 'natural capital'. But this would be possible if the model of development is socially equitable ecologically viable and economically efficient. And India's, unsatisfactory record in ensuring sustainable use of resources is partly attributable to the fact that the Government has been following a development model which is basically inequitous in respect of the distribution of the increased output of goods and services among different sections of the society. The ongoing process of structural reforms and the globalization of the economy is likely to further enhance the process of growing inequality in the society. It must be, however, noted that the Government has been carrying out certain programmes directly aimed at helping the poor and unemployed. The Minimum Needs Programme, Integrated Rural Development Progra-mme, Jawahar Rojgar Yojana, employment programmes for the urban unemployed, special women's assistance and old age pension scheme, etc. represent the Government's intervention for helping the poor. There are also several other schemes for helping the poor and the under-privileged like the landless labourers, small and marginal farmers, artisans and weaker sections of the society, such as, the scheduled castes and scheduled tribes and members belonging to the other backward classes. Even then ineffective implementation of measures like land reforms and imposition of ceiling on land holdings, distribution of surplus land to the landless, allotment of house sites to the homeless has failed to make any substantial dent in the inequality in the distribution of wealth. No wonder, the percentages of population lying below the poverty line both in the rural and urban areas are still quite considerable. In 1987-88 these ratios were

39.06 and 40.12 respectively as estimated by the official experts' group headed by D.T. Lakdawala.

The concept of human development according to the UNDP entails development of the people, for the people and by the people. "Development of the people means investing in human capabilities, whether in education or health or skills, so that they can work productively and creatively. Development for the people means ensuring that the economic growth they generate is distributed widely and fairly." Development by the people would mean ' giving everyone a chance to participate.' "The most efficient form of participation through the market," says the UNDP, " is access to productive and remunerative employment." So it continues to assert that " the main objective of human development strategies must be to generate productive employment." This is particularly important because contrary to the assumption that economic growth through increasing output would necessarily increase employment, over the past three decades, "the growth rate for employment in developing countries has been about half that for output" (Human Development Report, 1993, p. 3).

In India the same trend is reflected in the fact that the unemployment rate is still very high. In 1990-91 total labour force in the country was 314.9 millions and the worker participation rate just 37.6% only. Labour force participation based on usual principal status as given in NSS estimates indicate that it was 54.9% for rural male, 24.3 % for rural female, 53.2% for urban male and 13% for urban female populations (Economic & Political Weekly Research Foundation, 1994, p. 1232).

The development process in India has also been ecologically unviable in some vital sectors. The growth of output is heavily dependent on the intensive and extensive extraction of natural resources. The poor people are largely dependent on the sustainable use of resources around their habitats for their survival. But as a consequence of the ongoing development process they are being increasingly deprived of their access to such resources whose stock has been depleting steadily. For allocation of resources for production of goods and services the country is relying more and more on the market mechanism. But here the markets for both inputs and outputs are so segmented and amenable to manipulation by the powerful sections of society that the market mechanism leads to growing inequality and existence of idle resources including the human resource.

The technology used in some sectors of the economy is energy-intensive and labour-displacing. Chemical fertilizers, pesticides, insecticides, herbicides, etc. are being over-used resulting in pollution of water courses and contamination of agricultural, horticultural and dairy products and many other consumption goods. The industries are heavily depending on hydrocarbon or fossil fuels as the main source of energy and thereby causing fast depletion of these non-renewable resources and also pollution of the atmosphere. Only recently the Government has undertaken the programme of development of the non-conventional sources of energy seriously. India should undertake the programme of "resourceful use of renewable resources" more vigorously. Gowariker and Sachs have aptly claimed: "A bioma-ssbased modern civilization is not only possible but necessary and, in this respect, tropical countries have a comparative advantage" (1994, p. 1383).

Regarding the fuller use of India's vast potential of bio-mass resources the Approach to the Eighth Plan document outlined the plan of actions as follows:

> "To sustain social and economic development, especially in rural areas, steps are necessary to protect the remaining forests and to enhance the biomass resources, especially through development of wastelands. Realisation of the full potential of forests and wastelands in a sustainable manner which has substancial employment potential would be a key element to the revitalisation of the rural economy. Sustainable management of forests

> would require an institutional framework which would facilitate people's active involvement. . . . Every effort needs to be made to promote grassroot level participation in the task as part of a larger approach to the local area planning and development" (*op cit.* p. 44–45).

The National Forest Policy of 1988 also mentions that the main "aim of Forest Policy must be to ensure environmental stability and maintenance of ecological balance including atmospheric equilibrium which are vital for sustenance of all life forms, human, animal and plant. . . ."This policy declaration was followed by joint forest management policy resolutions by the Centre and States. West Bengal and fifteen other State Governments have taken up the programme of implementing the system of joint forest management. But the proposed new Forest Bill has been adversely commented upon by the environmentalists on the ground that it will concentrate more power in the Central Government in the matter of forest management and thereby the powers and privileges of the local people, particularly the tribal communities, in having access to the forest will be curtailed. But it is they who are directly concerned with the conservation of forests as they survive on that. Centralization in forest management may lead to more commercialization of forests and ultimately denudation of forests to the detriment of the local people's interests and ecological damages.

To stop the process of degradation of natural resources, empowering of people at the grassroot level for formulation and execution of local level plans of development is called for. The enactment of the 73rd (Constitution) Amendment Act, 1992 has made it obligatory for the State Governments to constitute panchayats at the village, intermediate and districts levels. Thus the panchayats will be able to function as the third stratum of government in our federal structure. Their powers include preparation and implementation of plans of development in respect of the following subjects:

agriculture, land improvement, implementation of land reforms, land consolidation and soil conservation, minor irrigation, water management and watershed development, animal husbandry, fisheries, social forestry and farm forestry, small scale industries, rural housing, drinking water, fuel and fodder, rural infrastructure, etc.

The tribal areas have been kept outside the jurisdiction of this Amendment Act. In the North Eastern States, where the Autonomous District Councils are in existence, they may constitute village councils in their respective areas. In fact some of them have constituted such village bodies. But the extension of the 73rd Amendment Act or a similar one to the tribal areas will give more powers and resources to such bodies. Therefore it is urgent that some legislative action is taken in this respect in consultation with the local people concerned.

An important feature of the Amendment Act is that at leaset one-third of the seats in the panchayats are reserved for women. Besides empowering women and improving their status in the society this measure will also promote the cause of environment conservation programmes. Being more directly concerned with the collection of fuel-wood and other minor forest produce and fetching water for meeting the family's needs they will be more deeply involved in the programmes of conservation of forest and water resources. [The author's earlier thoughts on India's approach to sustainable development are indicated in his paper on A Strategy for Sustainable Development of India (1996, pp. 182–192)].

India has miles to go in terms of women's development. The UNDP in its Human Development Report for 1995 has worked out a new Gender-related Development Index (GDI). Besides measuring achievements in life expectancy, educational attainment and purchasing-power adjusted per capita real income this index also includes the measurement of inequality of achievement between men and women. The greater the gender disparity, the lower the country's

GDI. India ranks 99th among 130 countries for which the GDI has been estimated.

Even more dismal is India's position in respect of Gender Empowerment Measure (GEM) which is calculated 'on the basis of disparities between male and female share of parliamentary seats, and between male and female administrators, managers, professionals and technicians and male and female earned income'. India's position is 101st out of 116 countries covered; India trails behind countries like Thailand (54th), Indonesia (56th), Nepal (73rd), Sri Lanka (79th) and Bangladesh (80th). The Report states: "Over the past 20 years, doors to education and health opportunities have opened rapidly for women, but the doors to economic and political power are barely ajar" (Quoted in the Statesman, Calcutta for 18 August 1995 and HDR 1995, p. 4).

It is in this context that the provision of reservation of seats in the Panchayat Raj bodies for women need to be endorsed. But more needs to be done. Such statutory obligation for accommodating women should be extended to the cases of state legislatures and the Union parliament in stages.

The concept of sustainable human development highlights the importance of the development of the social sector, that is, improvement in literacy ratio and educational attainment and health services. But the level of development of this sector in India is much behind even many developing countries. In 1992, according to the Human Development Report 1994 (p. 139), adult literacy rate for total population (as % of age 15 plus) was 50, for female population 35 and male population 64. Mean years of schooling (25 plus) for total population was 2.4, for female population 1.2 and for male population 3.5. For the period 1988–92, the position of health infrastructure and services in India was quite below the standard requirement vide, World Development Report, 1993. There were 0.41 doctors per 1000 population, 0.7 hospital beds per 1000 population (against the norm of 1 bed per 1000) and a ratio of 1.1

nurses to a doctor though the optimal requirement is 2 nurses per doctor. India has, therefore, to make much more investment on the development of the social sector than she has been doing so far for achieving cent per cent literacy and higher average years of schooling and substantially improving the status of health infrastructure and services.

Political Content of Sustainable Development

The effective empowerment of the people at the grassroots level to enable them to exercise control over the use of natural resources brings into focus the political content of sustainable development. Anil Agarwal has aptly pointed out (1992) that the achievement of sustainable development is crucially dependent on the society's ability to learn from its mistakes and to rectify them promptly. It is obvious that no society can claim perfect knowledge about the ecological soundness of its management and use of natural resources. Therefore the social and political order should be so structured as to contain the possibility of promptly learning from the mistakes and rectifying the manner of resource use. Such an order can be built up if the decision-making power rests with those who are liable to suffer the consequences of their decisions. The concept of sustainability is, according to Agarwal, thus related to hard political questions like the power structure determining the system of control over resource use and the extent of democracy in the decision-making process. Based on these premises he concludes:

"Sustainability . . . demands the creation of a political order in which, firstly, control of natural resources rests to the maximum extent possible with local communities who are dependent on those resources; and, secondly, decision-making within the community is as participatory, open and democratic as possible. The more this happens, the more we will move towards sustainable development" (*ibid*).

It might be possible to empower the community to have control over resource use and to make open and active participation of the people in the decision making process a reality through the effective functioning of the Panchayat Raj Bodies in India. But there must be the necessary political will for effecting genuine decentralization of power and ensuring adequate flow of investments for the development of the social sector.

Chapter 2

The Goal of Sustainable Human Development for the North-Eastern Region

Physiographical, Demographic and Economic Profile

The North-Eastern Region of India is very rich in bio-diversity and it is also an ecologically vulnerable area in the country. The region consists of the States of Arunachal Pradesh, Assam, Manipur, Meghalaya, Mizoram, Nagaland and Tripura. It has a total area of 2.55 lakh sq. kms., nearly 70 per cent of which is hilly, and a total population of 3.13 crores, of whom 26 per cent belong to scheduled tribes and 7 per cent to scheduled castes as in 1991. The area of the region comprises 7.7 per cent of the total area of the country and its population constitutes 3.72 per cent of the country's total population. The density of population (per sq. km.) in the region is 123 as against 265 for India as a whole. There are wide variations in density in the States: it ranges from 10 in Arunachal Pradesh to 284 in Assam, which is higher than the all-India average. Tripura has a density of 262 which is almost at par with that of the country as a whole. Such variations in density are accountable in terms of differences in physiographical features as well as the trends in demographic development of the States.

Considering the fact that about 70 per cent of the total area of the region is hilly and that the level of urbanization is yet quite low (only 13.89 per cent of the population lives in towns), the density of 123 per sq. km. in 1991 as against 104 in 1981 and 77 in 1971 and 57 in 1961 is indicative of the fact that the growing pressure of population on land and natural resources has been affecting the environmental health of the region. In table 1 a demographic profile of the North Eastern Region is given.

Within the region there are sharp variations in physiographical features. Part of the lofty Eastern Himalayas lies in Arunachal Pradesh, while the north-eastern hills of lower heights are found in Mizoram, Nagaland, Manipur, Tripura and Assam (Mikir and North Cachar Hills). The Assam plains cover the Brahmaputra and Barak valleys; Manipur and Tripura also have considerable areas of plains besides the hilly terrain. The region may be divided into the following three agro-ecological regions (Kanwar 1991, p. 12):

Table 1 : Demographic profile of the North Eastern Region

State	Area (thousand sq km)	Population (1991) (Lakh persons)	Density of population (per sq km)		Proportion of tribal population (% of total population)	Population growth rate %	
			1951	1991	(1981)	1971-1981	1981-1991
Arunachal Pradesh	83.7	8.58	—	10	69.82	35.15	35.86
Assam	78.4	222.94	102.4	284	10.99*	23.36	23.58
Manipur	22.3	18.26	25.9	82	27.30	32.46	28.56
Meghalaya	22.4	17.60	27.0	78	80.58	32.04	31.8
Mizoram	21.0	6.86	9.33	33	93.55	48.55	38.98
Nagaland	16.5	12.15	12.9	73	83.99	50.05	56.86
Tripura	10.4	27.44	61.4	262	28.44	31.92	33.69
All India	—	—	109.8	265	7.76	24.66	23.50

* For 1971. No census enumeration was made for Assam in 1981.

Source: North Eastern Council, North-Eastern Region at a Glance, 1991; and Basic Statistics of the NER, 1992.

(i) Assam, Manipur and Tripura plains
(ii) Eastern Himalayas, and
(iii) North-Eastern Hills (Purvanchal).

Although Arunachal Pradesh, Meghalaya, Mizoram and Nagaland contain mostly hilly terrain, they have also narrow strips of plains between hills and hillocks and in the foot hill areas. There are also sizeable areas of table land (plateau) in the Mikir Hills in Assam and the Garo, Khasi and Jaintia Hills in Meghalaya. The topography of the region is thus represented by hills, plateaus and plains. However, for the purpose of identifying differences in land-use patterns, the region may be broadly divided into the hills and plains covering respectively 70 per cent and 30 per cent of the total area of the region. Most of the hilly parts of the region are under tropical rain forest. Numerous tribes (numbering about 100) living in the hill villages practise shifting cultivation, *jhum chash*, for their livelihood. In the plains, settled cultivation is the predominant occupation of the people.

Since the planned process of development got under way in the region in 1951, some structural changes in productive activities and occupational pattern of the people have been taking place, it is true, but agriculture and allied activities still represent the main means of livelihood of the people. According to 1991 census report, more than two-thirds of the main workers are engaged in cultivation and related productive activities. The rapid rate of growth of population since 1951 and very slow pace of expansion of non-agricultural productive activities have been severely straining the carrying capacity of land and land-based resources and jeopardizing the environmental sustainability of the process of development of the region. For an understanding of this foreboding let us look into the environmental scenario prevailing in the region in the early fifties.

In 1951, 95.7 per cent of the population in Assam plains and 93.6 per cent of the population in Assam Hills (which included Arunachal Pradesh, Meghalaya, Mizoram and Nagaland) lived in villages. Tea plantation, which was started in Assam around 1840, led to the growth of a flourishing tea industry in Assam. But it was government-patronized expansion of a highly organized capitalist form of land-based and export-oriented system of production dominated by foreign capital in the background of a predominantly subsistence form of agricultural production. This sector did not have any significant spread effect and it was like an enclave of highly organized and high technology-using system surrounded by the subsistence and low-technology using system of farming of the indigenous cultivators.

The oil, coal, plywood and lime extraction (in Khasi Hills) industries were also there but Assam at that time was 'a peasants' land par excellence' as stated by Hem Barua (1960 p. 78). So also were Manipur and Tripura. In these States about three-fourths of the population depended on agriculture and allied activities for their livelihood. The cultivation practices are shaped by the village ecosystems. And the village ecosystems in the plains basically differed from those in the hills. In the villages in the plains the predominantly subsistence system of peasant mode of settled cultivation was practised while in the hills the primitive mode of shifting cultivation was practised.

Shifting Cultivation Model

Excepting for some minor details the *modus operandi* of slash and burn or shifting cultivation in hill forests was broadly similar throughout the region. Mixed cropping, that is, raising of a number of crops in the same piece of land in the given crop year, is an important aspect of this system of farming. Productive activities of the tribals dependent on shifting cultivation included, besides cultivation and processing of crops, animal husbandry, such as, rearing of poultry and piggery (some tribes reared semi-domesticated *mithuns*, (Bos frontalis), hunting games, collection of eatable and non-eatable forest products, fishing, weaving of cloth, making of baskets, mats, production of various handicrafts, agricultural, hunting and fishing tools, house-building, etc.

It should, however, be noted that the Jhumias did not produce everything they consumed. Therefore they traded some of their products with those of the non-tribals. The village council generally commanded control over the forest lands around the village to be used for *jhuming* by individual families. There was no individual ownership of forest land but each family selected its plot in accordance with the customary practice and any dispute among the families about the right of use of any plot was settled by the village council. Among certain tribes, such as the Kukis of Manipur and the Mizos in Mizo Hills the practice was different. There the tribal chiefs allotted lands to the individual families for jhuming, and they even collected some rent from the cultivating families (Hungyo 1987, p. 68). The traditional Khasi land system represented both communal ownership of land (*Ri Raid*) and private or clan ownership of land (*Ri Kynti*). The Khasis maintained village commons, such as, pastures and forests and sacred groves where trees could not be felled.

A typical jhum model of economy is a stationary one in the sense that the system reproduces itself at the end of every production period. Production is to meet subsistence needs only. The system yields output of goods just enough to maintain itself; it does not produce any effective surplus. There is no accumulation of surplus for 'expanded reproduction' and hence no growth of output from year to year. We may therefore call it a stationary economy. This is also a relatively closed system, for, this method of production does not entail any substantial use of inputs of production and goods of consumption imported from outside or disposal of produced goods outside the village to pay for imports and/or accumulation.

This system of cultivation evolved as the historical experience of the people and in harmony with the ecological environment. Subsistence needs were produced maintaining a long term equilibrium in the stock of natural capital by striking a balance between the using up of natural resources and allowing them to be replenished by the natural process of growth. It is for this reason that in the traditional jhum method of cultivation a plot of forest land once jhumed was kept fallow for a period of 10 to 15 years or even more. Thus the traditional system of jhum cultivation is a sustainable and least perturbing system of resource use. Therefore it ensures the preservation of 'a high degree of biological diversity'. Based on his extensive field studies in this region P.S. Ramakrishnan also asserts that 'the jhum farmer of the north-eastern India, as elsewhere, has always maintained his agroecosystem for centuries with optimum yield on a long-term basis, rather than trying to maximize production on short-term considerations' (1993, p. 366).

Though shifting cultivation was the most common method of agricultural practice among the tribes of North-east India, the system of settled cultivation was not completely unknown here. For example, the Monpas of Tawang in Kameng District of Arunachal Pradesh built terraces on the hill slopes for adopting settled plough cultivation to produce wheat. They manured their farms with a mixture of leaves and night soil. The Khamptis of Lohit district in the same state developed their own type of plough drawn by buffaloes and even by elephants. The Apa Tanis of Subansiri district have been practising the system of settled wet rice cultivation by adopting an appropriate system of irrigation on a sustainable basis (Ering 1969, p. 8–9).

Making an in-depth study in the system of wet rice cultivation of the Apa Tanis, Ramakrishna observes (*op cit.* pp. 51–52) that their valley land agroecosystem is exceptionally high energy efficient and sustainable form of productive land management. It makes use of nutrient wash-out from the hill slopes and recycles crop residues and organic wastes of the village for restoring soil fertility. An important aspect of the system is the optimization of water use in the rice fields through cooperative efforts of men and women under the guidance of the village headman. Rice cultivation is also combined with pisciculture.

In Nagaland, the Angamis and Chakesangs of Kohima district practise settled wet rice cultivation in terraces built on hill slopes. Some farmers even practise rice-cum-fish culture in the terraces where small pits are dug for holding water and fish fingerlings. During the rainy season, as enough water supply becomes available, the rice fields are kept in shallow submergence to enable the fishes to swim about and grow bigger. When water recedes they go back into the pits (ICAR 1981, p. 20).

In the Jaintia Hills district of Meghalaya, for the arecanut and betel vine plantations in the steep hill slopes, the farmers have devised the system of drip irrigation for which purpose water is carried from the source through pipes of split bamboo pieces (ICAR 1981, p. 18).

There are other examples of traditional concern for sustainable use of resources including forests by the hill-men in the NER. The maintenance of sacred groves and village commons is one such example.

Contrary to what the foresters and administrators allege, in stable population growth condition, shifting agriculture is an ecologically sustainable form of resource use as a number of recent anthropological works have proved (Gadgil and Guha 1992, p. 219). Since under this system production is for self-subsistence and not for profit and since its continuation depends on the preservation of forests, the tribal village authority controlled the access of the individual households to forest resources so that these could be used on a sustainable basis.

Such an equilibrium relation between man and nature breaks down when population grows fast, forest resources are used for commercial purposes and restrictions are imposed on the availability of forest lands for shifting agriculture as a result of which the period of fallowing is shortened.

The Decline of the Sustainability of Resource Use

As in the hills so also in the plains of Assam, where the subsistence system of settled cultivation was practised, resource use was of the sustainable type. In the pre-colonial period extensive areas in the Brahmaputra valley were under forests which served as the basic ecological infrastructure for the practice of cultivation. There was no individual ownership of forests, but the individual households had free access to forest resources for their own use subject to community regulation even though the Ahom Kings extended their 'prerogative of ownership over all woods, forests, ferries, mines, etc.' (Gait 1967, p. 270). During the Ahom rule some extraction of timber by merchants took place every year for export. The process of extraction was wasteful, yet the magnitude of loss of forest resources was not heavy. It did not affect the sustainability of peasant farming.

Environmental sustainability in the NER was threatened during the colonial rule for a number of reasons. Large tracts of forest land were allotted for tea plantations under the Wasteland Settlement Rules (Cambell 1898, p. 4). Encouragement was given to immigration of population and extension of cultivation by clearing of forest lands. By legal measures community control over use of forest resources was abolished and replaced by Government control. Reservation of forests and individual tree species restricted the area available for *jhuming* and thus affected sustainability of this system of agriculture. Commercial exploitation of timber was encouraged for raising government revenue.

Sustainability of resource use both in the hills and the plains was severely affected in the post-Independence period on account of the rapid growth of population and its increasing pressure on land and natural resources, destruction of forests for locating industries, hydroelectric projects, building of roads and towns and largescale extraction of timber from forests for commercial purposes, etc. Many of these have occurred in the wake of the initiation of the process of planned development of the region.

In this context it needs to be emphasized that sustainability of resource use cannot be an end in itself. The end should be expansion of human capabilities and the extension of the scope of choice of the people. The people dependent on shifting agriculture have few choices and the level on their capabilities is very low. Development of human capabilities is not only acceptable as a desirable goal in itself but also because without achieving this the environmental sustainability cannot be ensured in the long run. In this region, even before Independence the tribal economy was being transformed into a peasant economy under the impact of both endogenous and exogenous forces of change. This was causing the emergence of individual ownership of land and resources in replacement of communal control over individual access to such resources for productive use which was the fundamental basis of sustainability of resource use. Therefore, in any case, the system of shifting agriculture could not survive for long ensuring sustainability even if the planned process of development was not undertaken in this region. But the question that we must ask is how far the process of development has been one of *sustainable human development*.

Parameters of SHD

(i) Growth of Literacy and Education

One of the crucial means of enhancement of human capabilities is the spread of literacy and education. In fact, the UNDP in its very first Human Development Report (1990) included educational attainment or knowledge as one of the three basic components of human development, the other two being longevity (life expectancy) and living standard as measured by income. Originally adult literacy was taken as the measure of educational attainment but since 1991 it has been measured by a combination of adult literacy and mean years of schooling. This change was thought necessary to emphasize the importance of high levels of skill formation.

In 1951, in terms of the literacy ratio the NER was nearly at par with the all-India level (see table 2). Two hill districts, namely, Mizo Hills and United Khasi and Jaintia Hills were even ahead of other parts of the country.

The UNDP has laid stress on the 'dramatic improvement in the status of women' for achieving sustainable human development. It is, therefore, pertinent to note the progress in literacy ratio of both men and women. Statewise such data are available from 1961 onwards excepting for Arunachal Pradesh for which state information are available from 1971.

The 1991 literacy data are not strictly comparable with those of earlier censuses. For, in 1991 the question on literacy was canvassed for the population aged seven years and above, whereas earlier censuses covered those aged five years and above. 'Also, the 1991 census does not include the excluded younger population in the denominator for working out the percentage of literacy rate unlike in the previous Census' (EPW, May 14, 1994 p. 1229). Nonetheless, it has to be admitted that good progress in the literacy rate has been achieved by the States in this region. Female lit-

Table 2 : Literacy ratio in North-Eastern Region and India in 1951

State/district	Percentage of literacy 1951
Assam	18.1
Manipur	11.4
Tripura	15.5
Garo Hills	7.3
United Khasi and Jaintia Hills	6.8
Mizo Hills	31.1
Nagaland	10.3
India	16.7

Source: B.K. Roy Burman, Demographic and Socio-Economic Profiles of the Hill Areas of North-East India, 1970, pp. 18–25.

Table 3 : Progress in male and female literacy rates: 1961–1991

State	Male literacy rates			Female literacy rates		
	1961	1971	1991	1961	1971	1991
Arunachal Pradesh	—	17.82	51.10	—	3.71	29.37
Assam	37.3	—	62.34	16	—	43.70
Manipur	45.1	46.04	72.98	15.9	19.53	48.64
Meghalaya	—	34.12	51.57	—	24.56	44.78
Mizoram	—	60.49	84.06	—	46.71	78.09
Nagaland	24	35.02	66.09	11.3	18.65	55.72
Tripura	29.6	40.2	70.08	10.2	21.19	50.01
All India*	34.4	39.45	63.86	12.9	18.7	39.42

* Excluding Union Territories.
Source: Census Reports.

eracy rates in these States excepting for Arunachal Pradesh are higher than the all-India average rate of 39.42. But the range of differences between male and female literacy is still quite wide though in relative term the gaps have narrowed down in all the States.

The Working Group on Development of North Eastern Region during the Seventh Five Year Plan appointed by the Planning Commission found that investment on expansion of education in the region 'as an instrument of socio-cultural advancement' received special attention. This is evident from the fact that per capita plan outlay on education in the States of the NER in the Sixth Plan was approximately Rs. 178.48 which was higher than the all-India average. It, however, pointed out that the region suffered from 'qualitative backwardness in the field of education' because the wastage rates in the stage class I to class V were higher than all-India level. These varied between 68.3 per cent in Mizoram and 82.4 per cent in Arunachal Pradesh as against the all-India percentage of 63.5. Proportions of untrained teachers (in 1980–81) at all levels of schools in the region were much higher than those in the country as a whole. Moreover, enrolments in technical schools as percentages of enrolments in classes IX to XII were very low, that is, between 1.5 and 3.3.

In a society marked by illiteracy, innumeracy and extremely low level of technology of production and in an economically backward region as literacy drive is launched on a massive scale and educational facilities are provided by the state, productive capacity of the people rises; the process of economic development gets going. But after a time higher education of good quality needs to be promoted to build up a strong "scientific-technological base" and increase the availability of trained manpower for adopting higher and higher appropriate technology of production for achieving economic development. Higher education also expands knowledge in general which is so essential for social, cultural and economic progress.

In the field of higher education also considerable progress has been achieved since Independence, particularly after 1951. Now there are eleven universities in this region including two agricultural universities and three newly started central universities. Total enrolment in higher education courses increased from 61,580 in 1978–79 to 1,57,708 in 1990–91 (Table 4). This signified an increase of 61 per cent over a period of 12 years.

In regard to expansion of women's enrolment this region has achieved considerable progress. There are 22 Women's colleges—11 in Assam, 4 in Meghalaya, 6 in Manipur and 1 in Tripura—besides coeducational facilities obtaining in almost all the colleges in these states. Proportions of women enrolment to total enrolment in 1989–90 in different states were as follows as recorded in the Annual Report of the UGC for the year 1989–90:

Assam	:	30.4%
Manipur	:	33.7%
Meghalaya/Nagaland	:	38.8%
Tripura	:	37.8%

(The positions in Arunachal Pradesh and Mizoram have not been indicated in the report, but in these two states also percentages of women enrolment are not lower than that in Meghalaya/Nagaland, if not higher).

Table 4 : Enrolment in Higher Education Courses in 1978-79 and 1990–91.

Courses of Study	Arunachal Pradesh		Assam		Manipur		Meghalaya		Mizoram		Nagaland		Tripura	
	1978–79	1990–91	1978–79	1990–91	1978–79	1990–91	1978–79	1990–91	1978–79	1990–91	1978–79	1990–91	1978–79	1990-91
Ph.D/D.Sc/ D.Litt.			85	226		78	69	78						
M.A.		50	1591	2680	390	644	397	595		36	15	20	30	237
M.Sc.			749	1214	33	453	120	157				18	30	94
M.Com.			221	532		76		24				6	583	96
B.A.	199	1375	23280	71369	4938	13260	2508	4281	750	1733	636	2307	3789	6206
B.Sc.	21	58	8302	21241	1409	5440	621	1160	12	186	89	251	400	1748
B.Com.		90	4272	8522	74	680	696	513		112	173	408	1374	1750
B.E.			1547	2725									264	500
B.Ed./BT		23	1310	1179	139		279	467	60	132	106	69	114	204
M.B.B.S.			1911	1996	254	408								
Total	220	1596	43,268	1,11,684	5,977	21,039	4,690	7,276	822	2,199	1,019	3,079	5,584	10,835
% increase in 1990–91 over 1978–79		625		158		252		55		167		202		94

Total enrolment for all States in 1978–79: 61,580 and in 1990–91 : 1,57,708.
Percentage increase between 1978–79 and 1990–91 : 61.
Source: Selected Educational Statistics, 1978–79 and 1990–91 published by the Ministey of HRD as quoted in : North-Eastern Council, Basic Statistics of North-Eastern Region, 1980 and 1992.

There were 4 engineering, 4 medical, 4 agricultural and 1 veterinary colleges, 14 polytechnics and 58 technical and industrial schools as in 1990. Total enrolment in engineering course was 3225, in MBBS course 2404, in polytechnics 4165 and in technical and industrial schools 5734.

Impressive achievement in development of education in this region is attributable to, besides availability of financial resources for investment in education, the attitude and aspirations of the people as shaped by their socio-cultural values. Education reduces social and even economic inequalities. Therefore in a society which is having marked social and economic inequalities the upper classes seek to monopolize their access to educational facilities by depriving the poorer classes of their access to the same. In the rest of the country the society is divided into castes and into sharply divided economically privileged and underprivileged classes. The upper castes and the classes of people have been largely responsible for restricting the benefits of development of education to themselves. By this manner the inequality is sought to be perpetuated as aptly explained by Gunnar Myrdal. He says: "Monopoly of education is—together with monopoly of ownership of land—the most fundamental basis of inequality, and it retains its hold more strongly in the poorer countries. It does so even when attempts are made to widen the availability of popular education" (1970, p. 199).

In the NER the tribal communities are free from the pernicious caste system. Traditionally the access of the tribal households to land and land-based resources has been regulated by the community. Egalitarian ethos has informed individual and collective actions in the society. Even in the plains of Assam under the influence of Sankardeva's Vaisnava cult the caste system has not been a reckonable factor. Monopoly in land ownership has been also negligible in most of the districts of Assam. Similarly, Tripura until its integration into the Indian Union was predominantly a tribal state. After partition, large scale influx of displaced persons took place in that state which swept away caste rigidities among the immigrants. Moreover for the propertyless refugees, acquiring of education loomed large as the main means of earning livelihood. Thus the socio-cultural and historical factors combined with substantial flow of resources from the centre and the involvement of Christian missionaries and the Ramkrishna Mission, particularly in Arunachal Pradesh and Meghalaya, in running educational institutions, brought about all-round educational development in the region.

(ii) Life Expectancy

The UNDP combines life expectancy, literacy and educational attainments and income of the people into a composite index for measuring human development. Life expectancy is determined by a combination of demographic factors, availability of health care facilities, food security and nutritional standard, etc. The demographic objectives of significant reduction in birth and death rates and infant mortality, etc. cannot be achieved without enhancement of literacy and educational level, particularly of women. But, as the EPW Research Foundation has deduced from the comparative performances of the different States in India in achieving social development (1994, p. 1301), 'initial push to literacy and demographic achievements is a necessary condition for economic improvement but it is not a sufficient condition'. It is proved by the fact that even as Kerala has achieved high level of social development, its performance in raising income of the people has been a 'lacklusture' one. Kerala will need 'to harness physical and material resources to improve overall investment, output and employment opportunities' (*ibid*).

Not only in terms of literacy and educational attainment, in respect of demographic factors also the NER has achieved good progress by all-India standard. From table 5 it will be clear that both the birth and death rates in all the north-eastern states have been declining since 1981–83. In 1990–92 period birth rates in these states excepting for Assam

Table 5 : Birth Rates, Death Rates and Infant Mortality Rates in the States of North Eastern Region

State	Birth Rates			Death Rates			Infant Mortality Rates		
	1981–83	1985–87	1990–92	1981–83	1985–87	1990–92	1981–83	1985–87	1990–92
Arunachal Pradesh	31.2	30.6	25.5	10.7	10.0	9.3	81	81	71
Assam	34.0	34.4	30.4	12.4	12.4	10.8	100	107	76
Manipur	—	24.8	20.2	—	6.4	5.6	—	33	24
Meghalaya	—	35.1	31.3	—	10.1	8.4	—	63	58
Mizoram	—	—	—	—	—	—	—	—	—
Nagaland	—	21.2	17.9	—	4.6	3.7	—	23	10
Tripura	—	26.8	24.1	—	8.3	7.4	—	60	51
India	33.8	32.6	29.5	12.1	11.3	9.8	107	96	80

Note: (i) Crude birth and death rates represent number of live births and deaths per 1,000 of mid-year (respectively) population.
(ii) Infant mortality rate represents number of infant deaths per 1,000 live births.

Source : Sample Registration Bulletin, January 1994 (vol. XXVIII, No. 1) as quoted in EPW, May 21, 1994, p. 1302.

and Meghalaya were lower than the all-India rate. In the same period death rates also were lower than the all-India rate in these states excepting for Assam. Infant mortality rates in all these states without any exception are lower than the all-India rate.

Life expectancy data are available only for Assam. These are given in Table 6. Taking Assam's figures as representative figures for the North-East, it may be said that the life expectancy of the people—and that of the males and females separately—has been rising since 1981 although it is still lower than the all-India level.

In the sphere of demographic development, the most striking feature is the very high rates of population growth in all the seven states. Decadal population growth rates in 1971–81 and 1981–91 (vide, table 1 above) in all the States excepting for Assam were much higher than the all-India rates. The rises in density of population have been also significantly higher than the all-India rates.

Table 6 : Life Expectancy in Assam and India

State	Life Expectancy (1981–88)			Life Expectancy (1988–91)		
	Male	Female	Person	Male	Female	Person
Assam	52.4	52.5	51.9	55.74	55.23	55.47
India	—	—	—	58.1	59.10	58.58

Source: EPW, *ibid*, p. 1303–04.

Even as the NER has made some progress in the fields of literacy and education and enhancing life expectancy of the people, the performance in the field of improving economic conditions has been far from satisfactory.

(iii) Employment and Unemployment

In Human Development Reports for 1993 and 1994 the UNDP has specially emphasized the need for expanding employment opportunities for all people which is the *sine qua non* of pro-people process of development. This is required to ameliorate poverty and to raise per capita income—which is an important component of the index of human development. In Table 7 data about workforce participation, employment and unemployment are given.

Total workforce participation rates in Assam and Tripura are lower than the average rate in India. But in case of male workforce participation only the rates in Mizoram and Arunachal Pradesh are higher than the average rate of the country. Even then the position is quite behind the highest male workforce participation rate of 56.39 per cent in Tamil Nadu.

Female workforce participation rate is very low in the country. One of the reasons for this is the fact that 'a whole range of activities performed by women' is generally excluded from the purview of work. For the 1991 census special instructions were issued for avoiding gender bias in enumeration. But how far the 1991 census results truly reflect actual female participation in work is not very clear. However, female workforce participation rates are much less

Table 7 : Workforce participation, Employment and Unemployment

State	Workforce participation rates 1991			Employment in organized sector		Unemployed as a percentage of labour force (1987–88)
	Persons	Male	Female	Total (lakh)	Per cent (women)	Usual principal status
Arunachal Pradesh	46.24	53.76	37.49	—	—	0.2
Assam	36.09	49.45	21.61	10.47	30.5	5.6
Manipur	42.18	45.27	38.96	0.56	15.6	2.2
Meghalaya	42.67	50.07	34.93	0.69	19.4	0.3
Mizoram	48.91	53.87	43.52	0.34	23.1	0.1
Nagaland	42.68	46.86	37.96	0.66	14.1	4.5
Tripura	31.14	47.55	13.76	0.98	19.1	4.4
India	37.46	51.55	22.25	268.19	14.1	3.8

Source: EPW, *op cit.* p. 1306.

than that of males. Yet, excepting for Assam and Tripura in all the other states it is significantly higher than the Indian average. What is more, the female workforce participation rate of 43.52 per cent in Mizoram is the highest in the country. In the organized sector employment the share of women is generally higher in this region than that of the average level in the country. High rate of women workers in the organized sector in Assam is on account of the large women workforce employed in tea gardens.

Unemployment rates in Assam (5.6%), Nagaland (4.5%) and Tripura (4.4%) are higher than the all India rate of 3.8%. For the other states the unemployment rates are quite low. Since the economy of each of these states is predominently subsistence agriculture based, visible unemployment is negligible. For these States it is the growing volume of educated unemployment which has been causing concern. In December 1986 there were 12.67 lakh applicants for jobs on the registers of the employment exchanges in the NER. Out of this, Assam accounted for 8.12, Manipur 2.58 and Tripura

1.07 lakh applications. Number of applications on the live registers of employment exchanges does not represent the actual number of unemployed. But these figures indicate the high magnitude of educated unemployment. In the north-eastern states, excepting for Assam, the scope of employment for the educated youths is mainly provided by the service sector of which the government sector is the major component. In January 1988, numbers of persons employed in the public and private sectors in the north-eastern states were as given in Table 8.

The distribution of employment between public and private sectors is a clean pointer that if the expansion of the public sector is slowed down under the impact of the new economic policy, the problem of unemployment and poverty will be further accentuated.

The structure of production also lacks balance. In 1991 more than two-thirds of the main workers were employed in the agriculture and allied activities sector. In Industries including cottage industries percentages of main workers employed were 7 in Manipur, 2.5 in Assam and 1.95 in

Table 8 : Number of establishments and employment as on 1.1.88

State	Establishment (Nos)			No. of persons employed		
	Pub. sector	Priv. sector	Total	Pub. sector	Priv. sector	Total
Assam	4,606	1,654	6,260	453.0 (47.9)	492.2	945.2
Manipur	502	20	522	48.3 (99.0)	0.4	48.7
Meghalaya	613	136	749	56.3 (92.6)	4.6	60.8
Mizoram	437	16	453	27.1 (95.7)	1.2	28.3
Nagaland	587	111	698	66.0 (97.4)	1.6	67.7
Tripura	177	242	419	80.7 (89.9)	9.0	89.7

Note : Figures within brackets indicate percentages of employment in the public sector.

Source: Employment Review, October–December, 1988 as quoted in NEC. Basic Statistics of NER 1992, p. 116.

Tripura. In the other states this ratio was even less than 1 per cent. The remaining one-third of the workers belonged to the service sector. This indicates an unbalanced pattern of production structure which cannot ensure sustainable development of the region's economy.

Per capita income is one of the important components of the human development index. Per capita incomes at 1980–81 prices in 1989–90 (quick estimates) in the states of this region excepting for Arunachal Pradesh (Rs. 2199) were much below the all-India average of Rs. 2,157 (see Table 1 in Appendix).

Low Position in Terms of Human Development Index

In terms of social indicators the states of the NER are somewhat in a better position than many other states of India. But in respect of economic conditions these states are much behind the other states in the country. Therefore the human development index (HDI) as computed by the EPW Research Foundation for the Indian States show that Assam (only this State has been included from the NER) belongs to the group of states having low level of human development. From table 9 the position of Assam in comparison with a few select other states may be noted. Table 2 in Appendix shows HDI for 17 states.

Taking Assam's position as roughly representative of the position in NER as a whole, it may be deduced that this region is far behind the states like Kerala and Punjab in terms of human development index. Among the 17 states included in the study Assam's rank is 7 from below.

The UNDP has emphasized environmental sustainability as one of the reckoning factors in assessing the level of sustainable human development. Given the topographical characteristic of this region (70 per cent of the area is hilly), environmental conservation is of crucial importance in ensuring sustainability of the process of development of this region. In a recent report (1991) of the Forest Survey of India, it has been stated that while in the country only 11.51 per

Table 9 : Human Development Index for Assam and a few selected states

Rank	States	HDI	Per capital SDP at current prices (Rupees) 1980–81	1991–92
	Low Human Development			
1	Uttar Pradesh	0.1095	1278	4012
2	Bihar	0.1334	919	2904
7	Assam	0.2452	1200	4230
	Medium Human Development			
16	Punjab	0.7131	2674	9643
17	Kerala	0.7749	1510	4618

Source : EPW, *op cit.*, p. 1307

Note : Computed by using data on weighted average of male and female life expectancy, literacy and net SDP per capita based broadly on the methodology employed by the UNDP on their human development index (HDI) of 1990.

cent of the total geographical area is under forests as against the required percentage of 33, only in the north-eastern states forests cover more than 33 per cent of the geographical area. The report also claims: 'Demolation of forests due to 'jhum' cultivation has also been reduced from 73,410 sq. km. to 62,854 sq. km. between 1975 and 1984'. The report, however, notes that in Assam (Cachar and Karimganj districts) the demand for wood (24.35 lakh cubic meter) far exceeds 'the sustainable production of wood' (0.53 lakh cubic meters). 'Similarly the annual demand for wood in Nagaland exceeds the sustainable level of production by about 8,000,000 cubic meters' (*The Hindustan Times*, New Delhi, 21 February 1991).

Ramakrishna, however, points out that on account of 'increased population pressure and rapid depletion of primary forest cover' availability of fuel wood for consumption of the rural people in the region has fallen drastically and 'the villagers are now forced to trek 10–15 km. outside the village boundary' (Ramakrishna 1993, p. 4). Such a situation gives the signal that planned and earnest measures are required to be taken for restoring the stock of natural capital, preserving the rich heritage of bio-diversity and easing the pressure of growing population.

Obstacles to Sustainable Human Development

The planned process of development and modernization in the North Eastern Region has been mainly marked by the spread of literacy, expansion of educational and health care facilities, building up of the regional infrastructure, growth of urban centres, etc. Constitutional developments in the region, such as, formation of the Autonomous District Councils in tribal areas, emergence of Nagaland, Meghalaya, Manipur, Tripura, Mizoram and Arunachal Pradesh as full-fledged States, etc. have created scope for participation of a larger number of people in executive, legislative and judicial functions and exercise powers and enjoy privileges that were unknown in the traditional set up. An elaborate legal structure regulating the individual ownership of property with the right of use, transferring, letting and sub-letting and bequeathing of property has been built up. These developments have been widening the world view of the people and opening up the opportunities of realizing the fuller potential of human faculties and expanding the range of choice of the people in different spheres of activities. The philosophy of humanism and the spirit of self-confidence in the capacity for realizing higher aspirations of life have taken roots in North East India. This is a great positive advance in terms of human development, but it has not been an unmixed blessing.

The process of social and economic development entails a process of, what Schumpeter called in another context, 'creative destruction'. Some of the anachronistic institutions and irrational traditional customs and attitudes must, in furthering the process of development, give way to new ones conducive to progress. But what has been happening here is a kind of throwing away of the baby along with the bath water. The people are becoming more and more prone to abandon their time-tested and sublime values, such as, the spirit of sharing, ethos of egalitarianism, sense of dignity of labour, respect for equality of social status, etc. The traditional hold of the community in ensuring equitable access of the individual households to productive resources and conservation of natural resources has been waning.

The change that has been sweeping across the region should have some continuity. Otherwise this may jeopardise the sustainability of society which broadly implies "the extended and enriched reproduction of society in all its interconnected, integrated aspects" (Kabra, 1993, p. 215).

M.M. Thomas, a former governor of Nagaland, has blamed "the sudden transition from tradition to modernity without concern for continuity" for 'the good deal of demoralization' that is perceptible in the region. He, however, notes a silver lining in the cloud: "the traditional village base still remains intact at its core, though it may have lost its self-confidence" (1992, p. 6).

Jawaharlal Nehru had visualized such a danger. Therefore he wanted that "people should develop along the lines of their own genius and we should avoid imposing anything on them. We should try to encourage in every way their own traditional arts and culture . . . We should judge results, not by statistics or the amount of money spent, but by the quality of human character evolved." (Quoted in Ministry of Home Affairs, 1960, p. 13). In sharp contrast with this approach, all plans of development of this region are ultimately formulated and determined by the Centre. The North Eastern Council was set up in 1972 to promote and accelerate integrated development of the north-eastern States. Being a regional planning body it should have been an effective forum of the member governments to work out the plan schemes of inter-state dimension and the modalities of inter-state cooperation in carrying out such schemes with, of course, resources provided by the Centre for this purpose. But since funds come from its budget, the Centre exercises rigid control over the decision-making process in almost all matters.

The centralization of decisions-making process in bringing about structural changes has severely eroded the role of the community and the egalitarian ethos of ensuring equitable access of every household to resources like land, forests and water, etc. for productive activities. Easy flow of money for implementing exogenously formulated development schemes and other projects has been leading to growing corruption in social and political life. The region's natural resources are being depleted at a fast rate affecting the prospect of sustainable use of resources for improvement of people's living standard. The main beneficiaries are the contractors, businessmen and local vested interests. Economic stratification of the local communities is becoming more and more acute.

The system of formal education built up in the region is an exact replica of the one obtaining in the rest of the country. This has been giving rise to the problem of educated unemployment and, what is even more harmful, the downgrading of work culture. "The lack of work consciousness," laments Thomas, "has led to the wrong kind of leadership being provided by the educated to the rest of society. Aimlessness among the youth, drunkenness, drug abuse and related ills are spreading rapidly" (*ibid*).

In the tribal and non-tribal societies alike, the status of women is still far behind that of men. Literacy rate among women in this region is generally higher than in many other parts of India and their actual participation in work in the traditional as well as household sectors of production is quite high. Yet they have been excluded from participation in the society's decision-making process. In the tribal society it was a taboo for the women to participate in the deliberations of the village council not to speak of regional and tribal councils. Even today in the state legislatures, parliament and administrative and judicial services women's representation is minimal if not nil. Therefore a 'dramatic improvement in the status of women' must be given due priority on the agenda of action for achieving sustainable human development.

It has been noted above that even as the social sector in north-east India has been registering progress, the growth of production, employment and income has been sluggish. And it is for this reason that in terms of Human Development Index the position of the North East is far behind that of many other States: it is seventh from below among 17 States for which the index has been constructed (vide, p. 49 above). A significant drawback of India's process of development has been the trend of growing regional imbalances. The NER has been lagging much behind the pace of development of some other regions. The people of the North East feel frustrated and disappointed as the gap between their expectations and actual achievements in improving living standard has been widening. While to catch up with the other relatively developed regions of the country this region would require to maintain an environment of peace and harmony for the development process to be carried through without any hindrance, the region has been actually in a state of deep crisis on account of persistent ethnic insurgency in most of the States of the region. If the region continues to be in turmoil, the process of development will be severely slowed down and will further aggravate the feeling of frustration. Restoration of peace is a must for moving towards the goal of sustainable human development.

Chapter 3

The Strategy for Achieving Sustainable Human Development in the North-Eastern Region

Prerequisites of Sustainable Human Development

The basic principle of sustainable human development is that the process of development must be pro-people, pro-jobs and pro-nature. The priorities of development, therefore, need to be oriented towards enhancement of human capabilities through expansion of educational and health care facilities and provision of opportunities for productive employment and social integration. To make the development process a sustainable one environmental protection and regeneration should be an important item on the agenda of action programmes. This calls for maintaining a balance between human numbers and 'the coping capacities of societies and the carrying capacities of nature'. And, as the UNDP has asserted, 'Not much can be achieved without a dramatic improvement in the status of women and the opening of all economic opportunities to women' (Report 1994, p. 4).

We have already noted the growth in literacy rate and education in the north-eastern states. Though considerable progress has been achieved in this field, yet much more will have to be done to reach the goal of cent per cent literacy and to reduce the rate of drop-outs in schools, particularly in respect of girl students. The rural-urban and male-female disparities in the literacy ratios also need to be addressed. Education is the most potent means of enhancing human capabilities and therefore the need for universalization of education is of crucial importance in ensuring sustainable human development. This region is, in a sense, better positioned than most of the other States in India in respect of a favourable socio-cultural milieu for achieving this goal. Most of the communities here are free from caste divisions in society, and they have the tradition of having universal community education systems for training up of young men and women in the art of producing goods and services in their traditional manner and transmitting the community ethos and culture from generation to generation.

The critically important means of achieving this goal are the investment of adequate amount of resources for extending the facilities of free education to each and everyone and active involvement of the communities in formulating and carrying out of the plan of universalization of primary education. One of the highest priorities need to be given on investment in education, for, as Theodore W. Schultz, Noble Laureate in Economics has aptly observed: "The decisive factors of production in improving the welfare of poor people are not space, energy, and cropland, the decisive factors are *the improvement in population quality and advances in knowledge*" (1981, p. 4: emphasis in original). And population quality is shaped by education and health care facilities provided by the community for the individuals.

The community can afford to increase the volume of social investments, that is, investments in education and public health, on a sustained basis if it can at the same time continuously raise the earnings of the people through expanding employment opportunities. The process of development actually subsumes the processes of social and economic development which are interdependent. None of the sectors can advance on a sustained basis at the cost of the other. And the development of both the sectors must be people-centred.

Economic Development Since 1951

It is, therefore, pertinent to review the broad contours of the process of development of the region since 1951–52. At that time Assam, which included today's Nagaland, Meghalaya and Mizoram, was one of the economically most backward states in the country even as Assam is very richly endowed with mineral resources like coal, sillimanite, oil and natural gas, vast potential of hydro-electric generation of power and forests. During the colonial rule there was some industrial development but the industrial base was very narrow and weak. Tea industry was developed by foreign capital being encouraged by the Government which granted settlement of so-called waste land under most favourable terms. Other industries were petroleum and coal, total volumes of production of these products were not much. In 1951–52 there were 1,002 tea estates covering an area of 1430 thousand acres but the actual area under tea plantation was 389 thousand acres yielding an output of 340.4 thousand tons of tea. Annual production of coal was 50,000 tons and that of petroleum about 70 million gallons (Goswami 1994, pp. 131–150).

The development of infrastructure, which was built up mainly to cater to the needs of the tea industry, was at a low level. Whatever rail, river and road transport systems were built up were disrupted in the wake of the partition of the country in 1947 as the transport lines passing through the then East Pakistan (now Bangladesh) were snapped. Partition also threw into disorder the rural economy of the areas bordering on East Pakistan.

Besides the manufacturing industries in the organized sector, Assam has a tradition of a number of cottage and village industries, such as, handloom and handicrafts, silk, bell-metal utensils, etc. There are also some small-sized rice and oil-crushing mills in some towns.

Assam's economy was predominantly agriculture based. Even the tea being a plantation industry major parts of its operations were land-based. According to 1951 Census (Report, p. 102), 73.3 per cent of the population depended on agriculture for livelihood and 26.7 per cent on non-agricultural occupations in 1951. Urbanization was at a low level, only 4.6 per cent of the population lived in towns while 95.4 per cent in villages in the same year.

At 1948–49 prices state domestic product of Assam in 1950–51 was Rs. 204.4 crores and per capita income Rs. 258.6. Agriculture and allied activities accounted for 66.6 per cent of state income (Rs. 136 crores), mining, manufacturing and construction activities 16.1 per cent (Rs. 33 crores), commerce, transport and communication 10.2 per cent (Rs. 20.3 crores) and other services 7.1 per cent (Rs 14.6 crores), (Deptt of Econ. & Stat., Govt. of Assam, 1973, pp. 149–166).

Under the five year plans since 1951 substantial amounts of investments have been made for the development of infrastructure including the social sector, industries and agriculture. The industrial sector has become diversified. Many new small scale industrial units have been started. Total number of such units in all the north eastern states taken together has gone up from 991 in 1971 to 20,377 (NEC 1992, p. 122). Tea industry has grown appreciably. Production of tea has gone up from 1,50,370 kg in 1951 to 3,79,855 kg in 1989. Tripura is the other tea producing state where the production has gone up from 1,873 kg to 5,276 kg over the same period. Tea plantations have been newly started in Arunachal pradesh (6 units as in 1989), Manipur (2·units) and Nagaland (1 unit). In 1990–91 production of crude mineral oil in Assam amounted to 5,076 thousand tonnes and in Arunachal Pradesh 43 thousand tonnes. In the same year gross production of natural gas in Assam including Arunachal Pradesh amounted to 2,040 million cubic metres and in Tripura 180 million cubic metres. In 1970–71 total gross production was only 980 million cubic metres. In 1990 Assam produced 590 thousand tonnes of coal and 256 thousand tonnes of lime stone, Meghalaya produced 3,370 thousand tonnes of sillimanite and 273 thousand tonnes of limestone and Manipur produced 86 thousand tonnes of chromite (ibid).

Total installed capacity of power generation in the region as in March 1992 stood at 1,054.21 MW consisting of 424.81 MW of hydro, 552 MW of thermal and gas thermal and 77.40 MW of diesel power (*ibid*).

Whatever industrial development has taken place has not led to the proportionate expansion of employment. This is because the technology used, particularly in the large scale units, has been more capital-using than labour-using. In a study made by the National Council of Applied Economic Research (1960) reveals: "The average value of the OE (output-employment) coefficient for the entire factory sector of Assam is Rs. 3,544 which is the highest amongst the states covered. . ." This pattern has not changed much since, as the system of payment of subsidy in proportion. To the amount of capital invested in new industries in backward districts encourages capital-intensive technology. To encourage the setting up of labour-intensive technology, a system of subsidy linked to the number of workers employed should be evolved (Ganguly 1984, pp. 108–09). Of course, for achieving an industrial breakthrough a few fiscal and financial incentives are not enough, an appropriate structure of management ensuring people's participation needs to be adopted. Moreover, a sustainable industrial base cannot be built up without having sustainable growth of agriculture.

Excluding the capitalist tea planters, Assam's agricultural sector mainly consisted of small peasant farms using traditional sustainable technology. In the early fifties the net sown area accounted for 9 per cent and forests nearly 50 per cent of the total geographical area of the region. The sown area broadly represented the areas under settled cultivation and tea plantations. Nearly 50 per cent of the forest area was under jhuming including the fallow area under that system. The principal crops grown were rice, mustard, rape, pulses, jute, some quantity of millet and maize, short-staple cotton, potato, sugarcane, etc. Among the fruits produced the notable were orange, pineapple, banana, jackfruit, lemon, guava, plum, peach, papaya, etc.

In the pre-Independence period some level of locational specialization in the production of crops—agricultural food crops in the plains and horticultural crops in the hills—was attained. The hill farmers grew, besides some quantity of rice, various cash crops like potato, cotton, gourds, fruits, etc. which they exchanged for rice, salt and other necessaries of life obtainable from the plains. Such an interdependent economic relationship between the plains and hills also developed between the outer hill areas in Garo Hills, Khasi and Jaintia Hills and Mizo Hills with their respective adjoining plains in the districts of Mymensingh, Sylhet and Chittagong in East Bengal (now Bangladesh). But in the wake of partition of the country the free flow of goods between these hills and the plains (which fell in East Pakistan, now Bangladesh) was disrupted inflicting severe economic distress on the hill villagers near the border. Tripura which has a long border with that country similarly suffered dislocation in the free exchanges of goods with that country.

The findings of the three committees appointed by the Government of Assam to assess the adverse effects of partition on the economics of the border villages in Garo Hills, United Khasi and Jaintia Hills and Mizo Hills districts are worth noting. The hillmen in the border villages of Garo Hills district produced a small quantity of paddy but large quantities of pineapple, banana, jute, mesta, etc. and they exchanged these products for rice, fish, vegetables and other essential commodities of daily use coming from Mymensingh district of East Pakistan.

The border hill villages of United Khasi and Jaintia Hills produced plenty of orange, betelnut, betel-leaf, bay leaf, jack fruit, pine-apple, etc. which they exchanged for food stuffs supplied by the farmers of the neighbouring district of Sylhet. Some quantity of lime was also exported to Bengal.

Mizo hill villages adjoining Chittagang Hill Tracts sold cotton, sesame seeds, orange, chilli, bamboo, timber and cane to, and purchased food stuff other than rice, vegetables, clothing, kerosene oil, betel nut, agricultural implements, utensils, medicines, etc., from the traders of the neighbouring areas in Bengal.

The Committees highlighted the urgency of undertaking the task of rapid development of roads and transport facilities for linking the border hill areas with the internal trade centres. It was also necessary to help the hillmen to diversify their productive activities by taking to poultry, piggery, dairy and fishery farming, etc. besides cultivating cash crops like turmeric, potato, sweet potato, ginger, etc. The recommendations also included the setting up of fruit processing and canning factory units and development of village industries using forest products for making furniture, boat, agricultural implements, cart wheels, hand-loom, baskets, mats, etc. The need for establishment of fair price shops for making available foodgrains and other essential consumption goods like sugar, kerosene, etc. in the border hill villages was specially stressed by the Committees (Ganguly 1992, pp. 79–80).

At the time of Independence, the plains of Assam, Tripura and Manipur were self-sufficient in rice, which is the staple of the people of this region. Surplus of rice produced in the plains met the deficit in the hills. Some quantity of rice was even exported out of one or the other state. In the post-partition period, the heavy immigration of displaced persons from East Pakistan swelled the population of the region. There were also economic dislocations affecting agricultural production. With the commencement of the planned process of development in the early fifties inflow of capital, labour and administrative, managerial and other categories of personnel into the region took place on a large-scale. Number of urban areas and sizes of urban population grew substantially. Occupational distribution of population so changed that the proportion of non-agricultural population increased significantly. Such developments put a severe pressure on the agricultural sector as it was required to produce more food grains, pulses, vegetables and fruits to meet the growing demand for these products. Even as the total sown area expanded, yields of crops per hectare did not increase significantly and as a result the region became a deficit area in food production. The public distribution system in the region is, therefore, heavily dependent on food imports from outside.

North Eastern Council's Role in Regional Development

In 1972.under the North Eastern Reorganization Act of 1971 Meghalaya was separated from Assam and given full statehood. Mizoram was also taken out of Assam and made a Union Territory. NEFA became a Union Territory under the name of Arunachal Pradesh. Nagaland was ceded from Assam and given statehood even much earlier, that is, in 1960. Manipur and Tripura which were Union Territories, were elevated to the status of States. In 1987 Arunachal Pradesh and Mizoram got statehood. These States are economically backward and financially poor even as they are richly endowed with natural resources. For development of the different sectors of the economy by putting the available resources to efficient productive use the basic infrastructure, such as, road, rail, water and air transport networks, power supply, credit supply facilities etc. need to be built up. Development of these systems requires investment of huge amounts of financial resources which is difficult, nay impossible, for each state separately and alone to mobilize. Moreover, geographically these units are so located that the basic infrastructure requires to be developed in an integrated manner taking the entire region for this purpose as a single planning unit. It is out of this realization that immediately following the reorganization of the north eastern states the North Eastern Council was constituted in 1972 under the North Eastern Council Act passed by Parliament in 1971. It has its headquarters in Shillong, Meghalaya. All the seven states are members of the NEC. The main function of the Council is to formulate regional plans of development and get it implemented by the State Governments concerned or by constituting corporations. For implementing its regional plan the NEC receives plan funds from the centre which are in addition to devolution of plan funds to the seven individual states for implementing their respective state plans.

The NEC has succeeded in bringing about some development of the basic infrastructure in the region and some coordination in the approaches to development of the member states. But the pattern and level of instrastructural development is still far from enough for promoting balanced development of industrial, agricultural and other productive activities. Nehru wanted that 'people should develop along the lines of their own genius and we should avoid imposing anything on them.' But actually, the basic outlines of plans of development of this region have been decided by the Centre. Accordingly, the large projects-oriented development model has been in operation here for over two decades now. This meant not only transfer of financial resources from the centre to this region but also the influx of traders, contractors, engineers, educated job-seekers, skilled and semi-skilled workers, etc. The process of development has been bringing about changes in the demographic profile, leakage of income out of the region, sucking away of natural resources of the region and destruction of indigenous productive enterprises. This stands out as the most glaring example of the process of development of underdevelopment.

This trend has caused the emergence of local vested interests which have been gaining at the cost of deprivations of the common people. This sort of lop-sided development has been demolishing the traditional egalitarian customs and practices and patron-client relationships. Terms of trade between local products and products imported from outside have been deteriorating. All this has been causing immiserisation of the common people.

Whatever development is being achieved is sectorally unbalanced and therefore cannot be sustained. The service sector has been expanding quite disproportionately to that of the other sectors as more and more jobs are being created in the government offices without being matched by increased productivity. This type of development has obviously been giving rise to the phenomenon of rising expectations and increasing frustrations.

The problem of educated unemployment has assumed menacing proportions. But this must not be sought to be tackled by curtailing the scope of higher education. Rather some restructuring of the system of higher education in general and opening up of avenues for technical education relevant for this region in particular is called for (Ganguly 1994, pp. 341–365). The system of higher education should be conducive to encouraging the teachers and learners to cultivate the spirit of creativity. One of the objectives of higher education should be to achieve balanced development of the region which is rich in natural resources like minerals, oil and natural gas, hydroelectric potential, forests, etc. For this purpose the university system is to provide for what Galbraith says: 'sophisticated technical, scientific or administrative instruction'. And as asserted by him, 'it cannot come in isolation from the broad current of educational advance' (1983, p. 20).

Sources of Ecological Damage

The process of development of any region interacts with its biosphere (environment) as 'the human, financial, living and non-living resources' are applied to 'satisfy human needs and improve the quality of human life'. Essential ecological processes and life-support systems are, therefore, needed to be maintained as an integrated part of the overall plans and programmes for socio-economic development. The North-Eastern Region is a sub-region of the great Himalayan Region which is ecologically very fragile. Human activities over a long period of time have been causing deleterious effects on the essential life-support eco-systems, such as, soil, forest, fresh-water, etc. Unless the trend is halted and reversed the development process will not be sustainable for achieving improvement in the living conditions of the people not only in the hilly region but also in the adjoining plains.

The practice of jhum method of farming is not the only source of ecological damage in this region. The process of development in the region has been leading to construction of more roads and railways through the hills, building of dams (for irrigation and power generation) on the hill streams and rivers, expansion of urban areas, setting up of manufacturing units besides the rising rate of growth of population, both by natural growth and immigration, which have been affecting the fragile eco-system of the region. But in the case of road construction, dam building projects, location of large scale manufacturing units use of chemicals etc., ecological considerations involve mainly decisions on location and changes in engineering design, difficulties in the way of which are not formidable. The growing awareness among the planners and technocrats about the necessity of maintaining ecological balance may be expected to take care of these problems. What may be required is to make studies in the ecological impacts of the existing projects on the socio-economic life of the people for taking appropriate measures to avoid such changes as may be damaging to the human ecosystems. In any case, ecological problems on account of building of roads and dams, etc. have not yet assumed unmanageable proportions. It is, therefore, more important and urgent to consider in depth the possibilities of overcoming the problems of widespread soil erosion and denudation of forests and vegetative cover over hill slopes resulting from the practice of shifting cultivation and reckless uses of forests while carrying through the development process for improving the living conditions of the people.

Need for Controlling Shifting Cultivation

Shifting cultivation has been extensively in practice in all the states of the North Eastern Region since the remote past. In the present conditions of extremely short period of fallowing excepting for some pockets in the region, this mode of cultivation causes denudation of forests and soil erosion and keeps the cultivators at a very low subsistence level of living. In the post-Independence period, under the county's five year plans, several schemes were drawn up for controlling jhum cultivation and including the jhumias to take to settled wet rice cultivation. Besides the centrally sponsored schemes and state schemes some schemes have been formulated by the North Eastern Council in order to properly manage the watersheds for conservation of soil through jhum control measures.

Based on the visual interpretation of Landsat imagery pertaining to the year 1975 and 1984, the Forest Survey of India has recently proclaimed that the area of forests affected by shifting cultivation in the North Eastern Region has fallen from 73, 410 sq. kms. or 28.8 per cent of the total geographical area in 1975 to 62,854 sq. kms. or 24.6 per cent of the total geographical area in 1984. The biggest fall has occurred in Tripura, i.e., by 46.7 per cent, next comes Meghalaya where the fall is by 33.5 per cent. But in Assam the area has registered a big increase by 74.9 per cent and in Arunachal Pradesh by 7.3 per cent. Such variations from State to State reflect the differences in the progress of planned schemes for development of tribal villages in an integrated manner.

Even in the other states whether the trend will continue, it cannot be pronounced with certainty. For, the perspective of jhum control plans needs to be wider than what so far has been in this region.

The main thrust of all the jhum control schemes has been to make the individual jhumia families owners of plots of land where they can practise permanent settled cultivation. This has been resulting in the replacement of community ownership or access to land and land based resources by individual ownership or access to land. In other words, the primitive mode of production, which is less efficient but more egalitarian, is being replaced by the inegalitarian peasant mode of production. As a consequence of the peasantization process, the tribal society is becoming more and more stratified. Some households have become owners of land practising wet rice cultivation both by applying family labour and/or employing hired labour. There are others who practise both settled cultivation in some small plots of plainsland and shifting cultivation in the nearby hill slopes and forests. The third group of households still depend entirely on shifting cultivation. And this is the poorest group whose economic conditions are very precarious.

With the development of infrastructure in the region the isolation of the jhumias has been coming to an end. Development of transport and communication, roads, powerlines, progress in urbanization, extension of reserved forest areas, increasing areas of land coming under individual ownership or control, etc. have been confining the jhumias to narrower areas for shifting at the end of one operation of jhuming. This has been further aggravated by the growth of population. Repeated jhuming in the same plot of land after shorter intervals has been causing degeneration in vegetation and severly reducing the carrying capacity of jhuming. Since under this system, jhumias seldom have any accumulated stock, they become very vulnerable to natural calamities which are not infrequent.

Planned action is called for to control jhuming not for environmental protection and soil conservation alone but also for ending the process of growing marginalization of the jhumias who do not own any land but are wholly dependent on jhuming in the dwindling area of free but degraded forest patches. Therefore, the problem is not simply a technical one but also one of so planning socio-economic and cultural change that the growing process of pauperization of the jhum cultivators can be halted.

In the perspective plan for regional development equitable distribution of land available for wet rice cultivation in the valleys and of land on the mounds and slopes where plantation or horticultural crops can be raised must be ensured. The transition from the old to the new system means shortage of food grains for the tribal households. Therefore the development of an effective food security system is also an urgent necessity.

For building up of the food security system, availability of food grains as such will not be enough. Entitlement of individual households to their shares of the total quantity of food grains available will depend on their respective income-earning capacity. The enhancement of income-earning capacity of each household will depend on its access to productive assets and their uses for productive purpose. Since jhuming can no longer be a sustained source of increasing production, alternative systems of sustainable land-use for productive purpose will have to be adopted. The scope for such possibility may be widened by encouraging the farmers to turn to horticulture, plantation farming and silviculture in the hills and their counterparts in the plains to specialize in the production of food and non-food crops in their farms. Animal husbandry may, of course, be complementary operations both in the plains and the hills. But for this purpose sufficient area of land for fodder production has to be developed mainly in the hilly terrain.

The process of economic development is a disequilibrating process. Many tribal jhumias are bewildered and unable to adapt themselves to these changes. They are the worst sufferers. The only sure remedy against this is the spread of literacy and education among the tribals. Education not only liberates the mind but also prepares the educated for acquiring higher skills and higher productivity. Without spread of education, diversification of occupations cannot be achieved. And the future of shifting cultivators does not lie only in practising settled cultivation; they may take up many other productive occupations.

Education may serve as the bond of social integration. But the disturbances that are being caused to the human ecosystem in the hills under the impact of the exogenous forces of change could be better addressed by community response. As we have already noted, the system of individual ownership of land in the tribal villages has been eroding the community solidarity. Yet, the forests and biodiversity cannot be effectively conserved without the community participation in these efforts. And the community's involvement is crucially dependent on ensuring their access to natural resources to be developed on a sustainable basis.

Forest Development

Forest protects land from erosion and helps build up and restore soil fertility. But forest resources also meet the energy and other subsistence needs of the people. Therefore man, being guided by self-interest, develops and protects forests and thereby helps maintain ecological balance. But when socio-economic and political factors interfere leading to over-use and neglect of regeneration of forest, the balance breaks down as a result of which the poor people suffer the most. For them forest is almost the only source of fuel energy and an important source of food, building materials and various items required for cultural activities including rituals. It is for this reason that community forests have been an integral part of tribal village systems.

Since food-growing by cultivation of land is also an important activity for meeting subsistence needs, there arises the economic problem of taking the decision at the village level of how much land to be used for food production and how much to be left under forests. As the villagers had almost equal access to community forests they collectively took care of the community forests.

But this arrangement has been breaking down under the impact of various forces following the growth of population, private ownership of land and forests, market economy, etc. Now the tendency for using forest resources for private gains without caring for social losses has been gaining ground. In this context, a system of financial benefits to encourage afforestation activities becomes necessary as market forces need to be regulated to discourage felling of forest trees leading to ecological imbalance. The most critical consideration must be that those villagers with whose efforts and labour forests are protected and regenerated must be guaranteed benefits from those forests as and when possible. As far as practicable, community ownership and control over forest land outside the reserved forests area should be the basic pattern in the hill villages as that will be in the best tradition of the people.

The Rationale of Decentralization of Decision-making Power

Social consensus for sustainable use of resources has to be evolved through the political process of decentralization of decision making power and organizing planning process at the village and micro-watershed levels with an approach to autocentric development planning having a link with the larger economic system through the market exchanges of surpluses for meeting demand for goods from outside and relying on the public distribution system for meeting food and other essential items of consumption. The decentralized structure of planning has to rely on the people's knowledge system for striking a balance between growth with equity and conservation of natural resources. The decentralisation process should be a part of the more basic change in the planning process. The on-going paradigm of development which stresses on top-down decision making process and demolishes the traditional concepts of common property resources and community control over individuals' access to natural resources and marginalizes the role of the community need to be modified. The existing bias for bigness of projects and schemes and external impulses and inducements for change should give way to the smallness of projects to be identified and managed by local communities. The technology to be used should be as far as practicable local manpower and other resource-using and not such resources-replacing. Without letting the creative initiative of the people to have full play in the process of development it cannot be a sustained and equitable process.

In the plains of Assam, Manipur and Tripura the new system of Panchayati Raj bodies as envisaged under the Constitution (73rd Amendment) Act, 1992 may be in a position to make decentralization of the planning process a reality. In the other states and the autonomous hill districts of the aforesaid three states the traditional tribal self-governing institutions need to be empowered for undertaking the task of decentralized process of planning through people's participation. The Autonomous District Councils have achieved significant progress in protecting the tribal rights in land, formalizing the traditional and customary practices and undertaking some developmental activities. For a variety of reasons these bodies, of late, seem to have gone out of steam. Both the village councils and the ADCs need to be strengthened and supported for taking initiatives in undertaking participatory process of planning.

Such restructuring of the planning process will not, of course, do away with the need for state interventions in providing for the social safety net for the poor and the needy and for the basic infrastructure having inter-state dimensions. Therefore under the structural adjustment programmes the role of the North Eastern Council must not be underestimated. In fact, the NEC should effectively carry out the perspective plan of infrastructure development in the NER which will provide the social overheads for the decentralized process of sustainable resource use in the hills and villages for growth with equity to be a practicable proposition.

The Strategy for Sustainable Human Development

The North Eastern Region has made some progress in the development of human resource but it has yet to achieve much more and on a sustainable basis. Moreover it is not the end but means to expand the range of human choices. And this will not be possible without having growth of income through participatory process of planning. Every adult should have the opportunity of being involved in productive activities for earning income. The UNDP in the Human Development Report 1994 (p. 18) rightly asserts:

> "Economic growth, because it provides more options, is vital for poor societies, since much of their environmental degradation arises out of poverty and limited human choices. But the character of their growth and consumption is important."

The flow of investment for the development of the infrastructure including the social sector and raising productivity of labour through the adoption of sustainable resource-use technology and the involvement of the community has to be maintained. For fulfilling this objective three important areas of action programmes need to be specially emphasized: the region's rich bio-diversity must be conserved, women's status should be improved and employment opportunities expanded sufficiently.

Conservation of Bio-diversity

The North Eastern Region is one of the richest regions in the country in terms of diverse biological resources. But the on-going process of development marked by increasing rate of deforestation, raising of monoculture plantations under the afforestation and other programmes and overexploitation of bioresources for commercial purposes, etc. has been compromising the goal of conservation and enrichment of these resources.

Madhav Gadgil and P.R. Seshagiri Rao have outlined a system of positive incentives and taking of other measures for conservation of bio-diversity (1994, pp. 2103–2107). Conservation of bio-diversity should not imply debarring the tribal and rural populations from using these resources for their subsistence. In fact, traditionally these people have been using these resources on a sustainable basis and in the process they have acquired through experience over generations much knowledge about the biological characteristics of these resources. In contrast to this there are still gaps in the development of so-called 'scientific knowledge' about all such resources. Therefore it would be prudent to rely on 'detailed locality specific folk ecological knowledge'.

The Convention on Biological Diversity held in June 1992 under the auspices of the United Nations Environment Programme has also specifically highlighted the "need for respecting the traditional knowledge and conservation practice of local communities, especially women, and to share with them benefits accruing from the utilization of biodiversity" (*ibid*, p. 2103).

Gadgil and Rao have explained that the existing approach to conserve biodiversity by promulgating regulations which are administered by the bureaucracy 'in league with unscrupulous politicians and business interests' cannot be effective. As an alternative to this they have proposed "a system of positively rewarding the ecosystem people to sustainably use and maintain, indeed restore high levels of biodiversity employing flexible management practices fine-tuned to the prevalent local conditions through the length and breadth of the countryside. Such rewards could be in kind in terms of greater community rights over natural resources, in cash, or in terms of recognition of the value of folk ecological knowledge and practices of ecological prudence" (p. 2104). Ecosystem people include the rural poor including tribals who largely survive on collecting a variety of biological resources from their neighbourhood to meet their daily needs.

For practical implementation of such a scheme there must be some community level institution for directly managing the public lands, village forests, water bodies, etc. as well as for overseeing and coordinating the management of privately owned such resources. Panchayat bodies may be the appropriate authority for this purpose in the plains of Assam, Manipur and Tripura while the tribal village councils may serve the purpose in the hill and tribal villages where there are no Panchayat Raj bodies. In the caste divided and economically stratified village societies in the plains the collective decision-making process is not always conducive to the protection of interests of the poor and the downtrodden. But with the spread of literacy and the constitution of Panchayat Raj bodies through elections based on the principle of universal adult franchise, functioning of such bodies may be expected to be less biased in favour of high castes and economically powerful groups. The tribal villages are, however, free from social divisions on the basis of caste. But these villages are now becoming more and more economically stratified. Yet the traditional ethos of egalitarianism and community spirit still persist and these may enable the village councils to function for protection of interests of the villagers on a sustained basis without discrimination.

In the plan of conservation of biodiversity an appropriate approach to forest management and development of waste lands needs to be followed. The joint forest management policy, as already discussed above, emphasizes the cooperation between the community and the forest department in managing forests. Waste land development boards should also function in close association with the community organizations.

There is an urgent need for preparing inventories of resources down to the village level. Obviously, 'the Panchayat Raj bodies/tribal village councils and Autonomous District Councils may take up this task with the help and guidance of some relevant voluntary expert bodies. An appropriate "model for decentralised inventorying is that of panchayat level resource mapping pioneered by the Centre for Earth Science Studies in Trivandrum and the science popularisation movement, Kerala Sastra Sahitya Parishad. In this programme scientists work with village folk in mapping land and water elements, along with perceived problems such as gully erosion, infestation by weeds or lowering of ground water table on the village map at 1 : 7000 scale. These maps, and the dialogue initiated in their preparation is then expected to feed into planning of development schemes in that village area" (*ibid*, p. 2106).

In large parts of north east India village maps are not there at all. Yet the task of mapping out of the status of bio-resources in this region cannot be overlooked. This may be included as one of the obligatory functions of the panchayats and village and district councils. The National Technology Mission on Literacy has worked out a design of combining this function with the post-literacy activity. In such work Bharatiya Gyan Vigyan Samiti has been actively involved in some states. In north east India also such a model may be followed. In such task the local school/college students and teachers may be urged to take part. This may even form part of the curriculum.

Rich biodiversity of the North East may actually be a source of mobilizing financial resources for investment in planned development of human and non-human resources. Growing possibility of development of biotechnology has been attracting huge amounts of investments on research and development in this direction being made by multinational corporations, governments, universities and other research bodies. The corporate sector is keen on obtaining patents for the commercial uses of different bioresources as food, medicines, aromatic substance, fibre, fertilizer, pest-control device, etc. For this purpose the corporations seek to make use of the indigenous knowledge and expertise in these respects on payment of handsome royalties and various incentives.

"In this scenario," say Gadgil and Rao, "India is in an advantageous position with its high levels of biodiversity, its rich store of indigenous knowledge of uses of living organisms, and its substantial scientific and technological capabilities. It therefore makes great deal of sense for the country to launch a serious effort at conservation and sustainable use of its biodiversity resources. Such an effort would succeed only if it can draw in as willing partners its masses of ecosystem people, who for millenia have served as stewards of the country's heritage of biodiversity" (*ibid*, p. 2107).

What is true for India is also so for North East India which is a rich storehouse of biodiversity and has the long tradition of wide ranging uses of such resources by the ecosystem people who constitute a very high proportion of the total population of the region. The community's role in regulating the uses of natural resources here is still quite evident. And therefore cooperation of the ecosystem people in conserving biodiversity could be ensured.

Empowerment of Women

Any plan of sustainable human development in the NER must provide opportunities for women to play an effective role in the society. The women here are very hard-working and they bear most of the burden of the household chores and income-earning as well as non-earning productive activities. In the villages they collect firewood and other minor forest products, fetch water for meeting the family's needs besides cooking, rearing children and attending to all kinds of farming—agricultural, horticultural and animal husbandry—activities. They also work on the handloom and other cottage industries. Yet they are excluded from participation in the decision-making process even at the village level. Their representation in the legislatures and the government is very insignificant, if at all. Moreover, being overworked, they cannot give enough of their time to look after their children as a result of which infant mortality is high. M.M. Thomas has rightly pointed out:

> "Apart from the over-burdened women folk not being able to find enough time for their children, other factors like lack of getting potable water, fuel, inadequate supply of medicines and poorly run hospitals aggravate the situation" (1992, p. 6).

To remedy the situation there must be, what UNDP has stated, 'a dramatic improvement in the status of women'. Female literacy ratio in NER is generally high by Indian standard (vide Chapter II), but it is not yet cent per cent. Since population size is small, the attainment of hundred per cent literacy should be targeted within the shortest possible period of time. But mere literacy is not enough. Educational attainments of women must be raised by reducing the drop-out rates which are quite high among girl students.

Recognition of services rendered by women to meet the family's myriad needs as contributing to the family's income and state domestic product and as participation in productive work for census and other records is essential. Opportunities of employment in the organized sector and in the government and other public bodies for women should also be provided.

The principle of reservation of seats for women as enshrined in the 73rd and 74th Amendments to the Constitution providing for the constitution of panchayats and urban municipal bodies needs to be extended to the formation of elected bodies at all levels—from the village to the state and even to the national. Reservation of positions for women in public services will also help women to take part in shaping and executing government's policies and programmes. Such steps will help remove some of the disabilities of women.

The system of joint-ownership of both moveable and immovable property of the family by wife and husband may be gradually adopted with the concurrence of the parties concerned. Where the government allots land to individual households under different land settlement schemes, wives and husbands should invariably be made joint allottees.

Where possible, women's development corporations may be set up and special encouragement and help may be made available for women to form cooperative societies for organizing productive activities and enlarging the scope for women's cooperative participation in the development process.

Women in different states of the region at different points of time boldly and jointly protested against injustices meted out to them and against specific anti-women and anti-people policies of the governments as also violation of human rights by the peace-keeping forces. These experiences indicate the possibility of the women of this region to mobilize and organize themselves for asserting their rights in different spheres and participation in the community's decision-making fora. This process will, of course, be strengthened with the rise in women's literacy and educational attainments.

Employment for All

It has been noted in Chapter II (p. 46) that the workforce participation rates in Assam and Tripura are lower than the all-India average level while in the other states these are slightly higher than that. But employment in the organized sector in these states is much below the all-India level. The growing problem of unemployment both in the rural and urban sectors, particularly among the educated youths has already assumed alarming proportions. The problem of poverty is closely linked with that of unemployment. Taking Assam and Meghalaya's position as representative of that for the other states it appears that about 30 per cent of the population in this region was below the poverty line as in 1991 (EPW 1994, p. 1307). In the north-eastern States the problems of unemployment and poverty have a special significance. The basic foundation of the economies of these states has been the rural sector where lives 86 per cent of the population. The main productive activities in the rural sector are agricultural and other farming operations. Two- thirds of the main workers are occupied in these operations. Small-sized subsistence peasant farming in the plains and subsistence shifting farming in the hill villages dependent almost wholly on family labour had been the characteristics of the rural economy in the pre-plan period. Pressure on land was low and landlessness among rural families was almost unknown. The linkages of the rural economy with the 'rest of world' were few.

The process of planned development under way since 1950–51 and the population explosion mainly caused by immigration of population in the post-Independence decades have brought about basic structural changes in the north-eastern economy. With the development of infrastructure, spread of literacy and education and execution of planned programmes of rural development, etc. the isolation of the rural economy is almost broken. Market forces have penetrated into the remote villages. Self-sufficiency of the rural economy is almost non-existent. The equitable access of every household to land and natural resources for productive activities is nearly gone. Growth of landlessness and rise in the number of agricultural labourers in the north-eastern states are clear signs of poverty and unemployment in rural areas.

The centralized and the top-down decision-making process of our planning system and the exogeneously formulated programmes of development have been demolishing the traditional concept of common property resources and community control over individuals' access to natural resources as also marginalizing the role of the community. The region's natural resources are also being depleted at a fast rate affecting the prospect of sustainable use of resources and even causing irreversible ecological damages.

The basic approach to planning for employment for all in the rural sector has to be in tune with the approach to conservation of biodiversity oulined above. And in this direction the need for empowerment of the community cannot be overemphasized. The on-going process of development clearly indicates that sustainable human development in rural areas cannot come by riding on the piggy-back of large-scale industrial and urban area-centric development. The North Eastern Regional Centre of National Institute of Rural Development, Guwahati has highlighted the need of the North East to restore and sustain the basic features of self-sufficiency of its rural economy:

> "The fact that every rural family has some access to land is a great advantage which can be utilised for sustaining production. The disadvantage of the small size of land-holdings can be made good by reinforcing the other integral components of the subsistence economy to support and supplement production and consumption in the family. These components include livestock such as ducks, pigs and cattle; a grove of bamboo, banana, arecanut and coconut; a backyard fish pond, ubiquitous loom; all of which are common features of the subsis-

tence social economy of the region. All these constituents put together can make a viable asset base for developing self reliant and sustainable society" (Bi-monthly Newsletter, July 1995).

Such a structure of self-sufficient economy must not be a stationary one. The growth process has of course to be carried forward as without that expansion of the range of human choices cannot be achieved. As a corollary to the above simple model of organizing sustainable rural productive activities it follows that a substantial part of the initiative and outlay for the development of the rural social sector should come from local savings. But that will be possible only if local incomes rise through increased productivity in the farming operations. And caution is called for in choosing the technology. As Swaminathan has defined, ecotechnology rather than the indiscriminate use of green revolution technology needs to be adopted (see above, p. 20). The goal should be 'evergreen revolution' and not green revolution which has turned into 'greed revolution' in many parts of the country.

In implementing rural development projects just as rural savings arising out of increased rural incomes are a must so also the active involvement of the community is essential. The IMF expert Prof. Albert Waterston formulated a rural development model for developing countries based on the experiences of China, Tanzania and Israel in which he has opined that the beneficiary communities should assume responsibility for generating funds to support social overhead facilities. He has shown that "where governments have devoted considerable sums to social overhead facilities at the expense of allocations to improve agricultural production, rural areas have been left with schools without teachers, clinics without doctors, and chronic unemployment on their hands" (quoted in The Statesman, Calcutta 25 December 1974). Waterston has further highlighted the importance of "self-help" in his model. The other aspects of the model are: "labour-intensive agriculture, labour-using minor development work and agriculture-oriented small-scale light industry, using labour-intensive techniques with low capital requirements" (*ibid*). Such a path ensures self-sustaining rural development and flow of benefits to poor rural families whereas green revolution has tended to benefit the middle-income and rich farmers.

The village communities can organize soil conservation, land-shaping, waste land development, afforestation, rain-water harvesting, minor irrigation works, etc. and thereby create community productive assets and provide equitable access to these facilities to the individual households. Such works may be locally planned and executed by the community with technical help from experts, where necessary, for specific water-shed areas. This approach calls for both decentralization and de-bureaucratization of planning process. As the government intervention cannot be wholly ruled out in providing the social safety net, where required, rural works programmes in the slack season for providing employment to the landless labourers must be carried out, of course, through the active involvement of the local communities.

For addressing the problem of urban unemployment the process of bringing about diversification in occupational pattern and reducing the overdependence on government jobs have to be planned for. The process of industrialization and the development of basic infrastructure should be based on the availability and use of local resources as far as practicable. The technology used should be so chosen as to draw upon local skilled manpower which will be facilitated if the scale of operations is small. To bring about a shift from the use of capital-intensive to labour-intensive technology, government subsidy given to new industries may be dependent on the quantum of additional employment generated rather than amount of capital invested. The education system needs to be restructured in a way that the scope for acquiring appropriate skills and professional expertise by the educated youths is expanded to enable them to be employable in industries and commercial enterprises besides power-supply and other infrastructural construction projects. They must be also extended access to credit supply, subsidy and other facilities to be self-employed.

Conclusion

The model of sustainable human development has been related to the prevailing conditions and the needs of the North Eastern Region. It has been presented as an alternative paradigm of development to the existing one. But it must not be construed as a fixed prior formulation of action programmes. The emphasis on decentralization and debureaucratization of the planning process and empowerment of the community to decide what is to be done implies that the community organizations have to promptly learn from their experiences, and they must not shy away from admitting mistakes and reorienting action programmes in the light of the failures encountered. The new approach gives the local communities the power to control the use of resources on which they are directly dependent. But it is extremely important that decision-making within the grassroot bodies be as participatory, open and democratic as possible.

APPENDIX

Table 1 : Per Capita Net State Domestic Product at 1980-81 prices in North-Eastern States and All India Per Capita NNP

(Rupees)

State	1980-81	1989-90	(Quick Estimates)
Arunachal Pradesh	1561	2199	
Assam	1200	1650	
Manipur	1430	1702	
Meghalaya	1361	1515	
Nagaland	1383	1738	(1990-91, Derived)
Tripura	1323	1611	
All India Per Capita NNP	1630	2157	(CSO Estimates)

Source : EPW Research Foundation, National Accounts Statistics of India—6, Net State Domestic Product, EPW, December 23 1995, p. 3323.

Table 2 : Human Development Index for Indian States, 1990 (Arranged from higher to lower values of HDI)

Rank	State	HDI
1	Kerala	0.7749
2	Punjab	0.7131
3	Maharashtra	0.6430
4	Haryana	0.5995
5	Gujarat	0.5453
6	Tamil Nadu	0.4873
7	Karnataka	0.4772
8	West Bengal	0.4176
9	Himachal Pradesh	0.4005
10	Andhra Pradesh	0.3397
11	Assam	0.2452
12	Rajasthan	0.2294
13	Orissa	0.2132
14	Madhya Pradesh	0.1863
15	Bihar	0.1334
16	Uttar Pradesh	0.1095
17	Jammu & Kashmir	0.1001

Source : EPW Research Foundation, Human Development Index for Indian States, EPW, May 21, 1994, p. 1307, Table 5 (b). HDI has been computed by "using data on weighted average of male and and female life expectancy, literacy and net SDP per capita based broadly on the methodology employed by the UNDP on their hiuman development index (HDI) of 1990."

A NOTE ON ESTIMATION OF HDI

Human development index measures the extent of deprivation of the people of a country/state. For estimating the extent of deprivation of an average person of a country in respect of life expectancy, education and income, the UNDP identifies minimum achievements worldwide, that is, the lowest national life expectancy, lowest national level of adult literacy and lowest national level of inocme per capita. As against that 'a maximum or desirable or adequate level of attainment' is also worked out. For the 1991 Human Development Report, the HDI was constructed in three steps. "The first step was to define a country's measure of deprivation for each of the three variables—life expectancy (X_1), literacy (X_2) and (the log of) per capita GDP(X_3). A maximum and a minimum value was identified for the actual values of each of the three variables. The deprivation measure then placed the country in the 0–1 range defined by the difference between the maximun and the minimum. Thus I_{ij} was the deprivation indicator for the jth country with respect to the ith variable, defined as :

$$I_{ij} = \frac{\left(\max_j Xij - Xij\right)}{\left(\max_j Xij - \min_j Xij\right)}$$

"The second step was to define an average deprivation indicator, (Ij), by taking a simple average of the three indicators :

$$I_j = \frac{1}{3}\sum_{i=1}^{3} I_{ij}$$

"The third step was to measure the human development index (HDI) as one minus the average deprivation index :

$$(HDI)_j = (1\text{-}I_j)$$

(*Human Development Report*, 1991, p. 88)

According to this estimate in 1990 HDI for India was 0.309 and the country's rank was 134 among 173 countries. Japan topped the list with HDI of 0.983, while Guinea was at the bottom of the list having HDI of 0.045."

Bibliography

1. Agarwal, Anil, 1992. What is Sustainable Development? Published in *Down to Earth*, 15 June, reproduced in *The Administrator, Mussoorie*, Special Volume on Sustainable development.
2. Barua, Hem, 1960. *The Red River and the Blue Hill*, Guwahati.
3. Bhalla, G.S., 1994. India's Agricultural Policy for the Coming Decades, paper presented at *National Seminar on Population and Agricultural Policy: India 2020* organized by the Institute for Studies in Population, Agriculture and Rural Change, University of Kalyani, Kalyani, West Bengal.
4. Campbell, T.J., 1898. Brief History of the Forest Department in Assam, published in Home, A.L., *Assam Forest Manual containing the Assam Forest Regulation of 1891 and other documents*.
5. Daly, Herman E. 1977. 'The Steady-state Economy: What, Why, and How' published in Dennis Clark Pirages (ed.), *The Sustainable Society: Implications for Limited Growth* Praeger Publishers, New York.
6. Daly, Herman E., 1979. Ethical Implications of Limits to Global Development, published in William M. Finnin, Jr. and Gerald Alonzo Smith (eds.), *The Morality of Scarcity*, Louisiana State University Press, USA.
7. Ering, D., 1969. 'North-East Frontier Agency' published in K.S. Singh (ed), *The Tribal Situation in India*, Indian Institute of Advanced Study, Shimla, 1992 (second reprint).

8. Economic and Political Weekly Research Foundation, 1994. Social Indicators of Development, *Economic and Political Weekly*, 14 and 21 May, 1994.
9. Finnin, W.M. (Jr.) and Smith, G.A. (editors), 1979. *The Morality of Scarcity, Limited Resources and Social Policy*, Louisiana State University Press, London.
10. Gadgil, M. and Guha, R. 1992. *This fissured Land: An Ecological History of India*, Delhi.

10a. Gadgil, M. and Rao, P.R. Seshagiri, 1994. A System of Positive Incentives to Conserve Biodiversity, *Economic and Political Weekly*, 6 August, PP. 2103–2107

11. Gait, E., 1967. *A History of Assam*, Revised and Enlarged by Barua, B.K. and Murthy, H.V.S., Calcutta.
12. Galbraith, J.K., 1983. *Essays from the Poor to the Rich*, Bharatiya Vidya Bhavan, Bombay.
13. Ganguly, J.B., 1984. Economic Development and Social Tension in the Northeastern Region, Published in *North-east Region: Problems and Prospects of Development*, Ed. B.L. Abbi, Centre for Research in Rural and Industrial Development, Chandigarh.
14. Ganguly J.B., 1987. Projections of Land-Use Pattern and land-based Occupations in North-Eastern Region in 2000 A.D. published in B. Datta Ray (ed), *North-East India 2000 A.D.*, Delhi.
15. Ganguly J.B., 1992. Zonal Planning in Agriculture and Allied Activities, published in Adiseshiah, Malcolm S. (ed) *Planning Perspectives for the North-Eastern and Eastern Zone*, India International Centre, Delhi.
16. Ganguly J.B., 1994. Towards Integrated Development of University Education in India's North Eastern Region, published in Mathur, M.V., Arora, R.K., and Sogani, M. (ed) *Indian University System: Revitalization and Reform*, Wiley Eastern Ltd., New Delhi.
17. Ganguly, J.B. 1996. A Strategy for Sustainable Development of India, published in S.P. Shukla and Nandshwar Sharma (eds), *Sustainable Developmental Strategy* (India Context), Mittal Publications, New Delhi.

18. Goswami, P.C., 1994. *The Economic Development of Assam*, Third Revised edition, Kalyani Publishers, Ludhiana.
19. Government of Assam, 1973. *Statistical Handbook, Assam*, compiled by the Department of Economics and Statistics, Guwahati.
20. Government of India, 1960. *Report of the Committee on Special Multipurpose Tribal Blocks*, Ministry of Home Affairs, New Delhi.
21. Government of India, Ministry of Environment and Forests 1988, *National Forest Policy*, 1988.
22. Gowariker, V. and Sachs, Ignacy, 1994. 'Redefining the Good Society: A North-South Dialogue on Challenges of 21st Century' published in *Economic and Political Weekly*, 4 June, pp. 1383–1385.
23. Hungya, P., 1987. Land Tenure System in the Hills of Manipur, published in Datta, B.B. and Karna, M.N. (ed) *Land Relations in North-East India*, People's Publishing House, New Delhi.
24. Indian Council of Agricultural Research, North-Eastern Region, Shillong, 1981. *Water Management in North Eastern Hill Region*, Shillong.
25. Kabra, K.N., 1993. Crises, Maladjustment and Sustainability of Development: Some Initial Explorations, published in *The Indian Journal of Public Administration*, Vol. XXXIX No. 3 (Special Issue on Towards Sustainable Development of Society Imperatives and Perspectives), Delhi.
26. Kanwar, J.S., 1991. *Indian Agriculture at Cross-Roads, Challenges and Strategies*, Lal Bahadur Shastri Memorial Lecture at Indian Agricultural Research Institute, New Delhi.
27. Meadows, Donella H. et al. 1979. *The Limits to Growth*, A Report for the club of Rome's Project on the predicament of Mankind (Second Edition), Universe Books, New York.
28. Myrdal, Gunnar, 1970. *The Challenge of World Poverty*, Penguin, Great Britain.

29. National Council of Applied Economic Research, 1960 Delhi. *A Study on Regional Differences in Industrial Pattern.*
30. National Institute of Rural Development, NE 1995. *Seven Sisters*: Bimonthly Newsletter, July. Regional Centre, Guwahati
31. Nayar, K.R. 1994. Politics of 'Sustainable Development', *Economic and Political Weekly*, 28 May, pp. 1327–29.
32. Planning Commission, Govt. of India. *Sixth Five Year Plan 1980–85.*
33. Planning Commission, Govt. of India. *Seventh Five Year Plan, 1985–90*, Mid-term Appraisal.
34. Planning Commission, Govt. of India. *Approach to the Eighth Five Year Plan*, 1990–95.
35. Raza, Moonis, 1990. Towards Sustainable Development, Published in *Think India*, Vol. 2, No. 2.
36. Ramakrishna, P.S., 1993. *Shifting Agriculture and Sustainable Development*, Oxford Univ. Press, Delhi.
37. *Report on the Symposium On Sustainable Consumption* held at Oslo, Norway, 19–20 January, 1994.
38. Roy Burman, B.K., 1970. *Demographic and Socio-Economic Profiles of the Hill Areas of North-East India*, Office of the Registrar General, Govt. of India, New Delhi.
39. Schultz, T.W., 1981. *Investing in People: The Economics of Population Quality*, Hindustan Publishing Corporation (India), Delhi.
40. Shiva Bandana, 1993. Monocultures of the Mind—Understanding the Threats to Biological and Cultural Diversity, published in the *Indian Journal of Public Administration*, op. cit.
41. Suraiya, J., 1984. Championing the Cause of Conservation, *The Statesman*, Calcutta, 3 December.
42. Swaminathan, M.S., 1995. Towards an Evergreen Revolution, Published in *the Hindu*, Sunday Magazine, 21 May, Delhi.
43. *The Statesman*, Calcutta, 1974. IMF Study says: *Beneficiaries should Pay for Rural Uplift* : Reproduction of part of the

article of Prof. Albert Waterston Published in the IMF's journal, Finance and Development, December.

44. Thomas, M.M., 1992. N-E: Developing the Human Potential, published in the *Times of India*, Delhi, 23 April.
45. United Nations, Development Programme (UNDP), *Human Development Report*, for 1991, 1992, 1993, 1994 and 1995 Oxford University Press.
46. The World Bank, 1993. *World Development Report*, 1993, Oxford University Press.

Index